ANCIENT GREEK DRAMA
IN BRIEF

GIORGOS CANONIS

ANCIENT GREEK DRAMA
IN BRIEF

TRANSLATION:
VASSILIOS MANIMANIS

EDITING:
STEVE COWMAN
LEDA DELIGIANNAKIS

DIAVLOS
ATHENS 2010

Giorgos Canonis
ANCIENT GREEK DRAMA IN BRIEF
Copyright© 2010 by DIAVLOS PUBLICATIONS
95 Alexandreias & Timaiou str.
(Archaeological Site of Plato's Academy)
10441, Athens, Greece
Tel.: +30 210 3631169, +30 210 3625315
FAX: +30 210 3617473
e-mail: info@diavlos-books.gr

www.diavlosbooks.com

ISBN: 978-960-531-265-7

COVER & INTERIOR DESIGN: DIAVLOS PUBLICATIONS

To Sophia

CONTENTS

INTRODUCTION

As with its predecessors, the Greek editions of *Ancient Greek Comedies In Brief* and *Ancient Greek Tragedies In Brief,* this book is not necessarily intended to be read from cover to cover. Although it constitutes a fascinating collection of stories, it can also be used as a reference for those readers who want to become familiar with the details of a play.

Rather than reading a play in its entirety, this book also offers a convenient alternative to those wishing to obtain a better knowledge of the plot before attending a production. The clear and detailed descriptions will allow the reader to follow and enjoy a play even if performed in a foreign language.

Whilst by no means a replacement of the original texts, *Ancient Greek Drama In Brief* provides an accessible introduction to these works which are of fundamental importance to Western literature.

TRAGEDIES

A G A M E M N O N – Oresteia, part I
(Aeschylus)

We are in Argos, in Agamemnon's palace. On the palace roof a guard is watching the opposite shore across the water, waiting for a victorious signal indicating that Troy has been conquered at last. A chorus of old men who have remained in Argos during the war stands in front of the palace.

The elders report events that have taken place during the ten years of the war. They are talking about how Agamemnon was asked to give his daughter, Iphigenia, to be sacrificed in order to placate the goddess Artemis who was keeping the Achaean fleet in Aulis. Although it caused him deep sorrow, the king and commander had come to terms with the decision he had taken.

Clytemnestra, Agamemnon's wife and queen, appears and announces that Troy has finally fallen. She has been informed by the signals sent by her husband who used a series of successive fires lit on the mountaintops from Troy to Argos.

The queen departs from the scene and a herald appears, announcing to the people of Argos that their king will shortly arrive, victorious. Indeed, Agamemnon then appears on a chariot together with his slave Cassandra, the daughter of the king of Troy.

The chorus declares their loyalty to the king, yet they warn him that some people did not behave well during his absence.

Clytemnestra appears again, declaring her love and telling of her sleepless nights while waiting for Agamemnon's return. She informs him that she has sent their son Orestes to their friend Strophius, in order to protect him from a potential revolt in the city had Agamemnon died in Troy. She is excessive in her emotional display, deploying red carpets for her husband to approach and enter the palace. Agamemnon fears this honour, only fit for gods, but Clytemnestra insists and finally persuades him. Descending from the chariot, he presents Cassandra to his wife and asks her to treat her with kindness.

Clytemnestra orders Cassandra to go inside and stand by the altars along with the other slaves. Cassandra, who is in a state of ecstasy, does not reply to her and Clytemnestra leaves the stage in fury. A wailing Cassandra then delivers a prophecy that both she and Agamemnon will be killed by Clytemnestra. She then narrates her personal story, telling the audience that her bad fortune began when, after falling in love with her, god Apollo gave her the gift of prophecy. Cassandra rejected him and Apollo cursed her so that nobody warned with her prophecies would believe her. She continues by foretelling Orestes' revenge by killing his own mother, and enters the palace.

Moans are heard and after a while Clytemnestra appears. Full of pride, she announces that she just killed Agamemnon with her own bare hands; as he was leaving the bathroom, she threw a cloth over him to trap him and then stabbed him with a sword three times, leaving him dead. Beside him, she also killed Cassandra. The chorus disapproves. She defends her actions by saying that this was her revenge for the sacrifice of her daughter Iphigenia. She asks them to remember that horrible event and to accept that she, as a mother, acted rightly. She adds that Agamemnon had not been faithful to her and became involved with Chryseis and other slaves whilst in Troy. And as if this was not enough, he has also brought his lover Cassandra back to Argos with him, who now also lays in the palace dead. The chorus men do not accept her reasoning and warn her that she will pay for the murders, whilst wailing for their lost king.

Aegisthus appears. He tells his own story and speaks about his reasons for revenge: Agamemnon's father had killed his brothers and had offered their flesh for dinner to his father Thyestes. As for Aegisthus himself, who was a baby at the time, he was exiled by Agamemnon. The murder of Agamemnon, planned by him and executed by Clytemnestra, was his revenge. He would now marry Clytemnestra and ruthlessly rule the kingdom run by the dynasty of the Atreides. The chorus accuses Aegisthus of committing a murder using "a woman's hands" and warns him that he will find them opposed to the tough rule he plans. He, in turn, threatens that they will pay dearly for their disrespect.

The tragedy ends with Clytemnestra promising that she will support him and assuring him that no obstacle which they cannot confront together will get in their way.

A J A X
(SOPHOCLES)

In front of Ajax's tent, Odysseus stands accompanied by goddess Athena. Odysseus tells the goddess that cattle herds have been found slaughtered and that their keepers were also found dead with them. Odysseus is in front of his adversary's tent because he believes that Ajax has committed the slaughter, as he was seen rushing through the fields with blood dripping from his sword. Athena confirms Ajax's guilt. The reason for his act was his wrath against the Argives and their leaders, Agamemnon and Menelaus, who had given the weapons of the dead hero Achilles to Odysseus and not to him. When Ajax went out to kill the Argives, Athena temporarily maddened him and led him to the cowsheds instead of the Atreides' tents. As he was slaughtering the animals he believed that he was slaying Agamemnon and Menelaus.

The goddess calls Ajax out of his tent, assuring Odysseus he has nothing to fear as following her divine intervention Ajax will not be able to see him. Ajax tells Athena that he killed the Atreides, who had disgraced him, and that inside his tent was Odysseus, whom he will whip to death. Athena gives him permission to do as he wishes, and Ajax leaves the stage asking her to remain his ally forever. Odysseus stays alone with the goddess, and while up to now he considered Ajax as his adversary he now feels sorrow for his current state. Athena warns Odysseus not to speak badly of the gods as Ajax did, nor to take pride in his power or riches, because a single day is enough for someone to be humiliated by the gods.

The chorus of Salaminian sailors appears. They express their compassion for their king and say they are certain that some god maddened Ajax and led him to commit these insane and violent acts.

Then Ajax's slave and lover, Tecmessa, appears lamenting the mental state of the king and describing how Ajax went out of his tent during the night and returned bringing animals back, which he tortured and slaughtered. When his delirium passed and he saw what he had done, he asked her to describe his actions to him and then, deeply ashamed, asked to be left alone.

Ajax is heard moaning and shouting that following his actions he does not want to live anymore. He, the bravest of all, fell victim to goddess Athena, who manipulated his mind. He is unsure of what to do, but what he is sure of is that a noble person must either live honestly or die in honour. The chorus compassionately asks him to forget what took place, since there is nothing that can now be done to change it. Ajax asks for Eurysaces, his son with Tecmessa to be brought in. He speaks to him and from his words it becomes apparent that he wants to commit suicide but then changes his mind. He decides to go to the seashore to cleanse himself, hoping that this way he will free himself of the wrath of the goddess. He will then bury the sword he used for his shameful deeds deep in the ground. This sword had been given to him by his enemy, Hector the Trojan, and since then only bad things had happened to him. He acknowledges his mistakes and admits that he must always retreat before the gods and honour the Atreides. The men of the chorus agree with his words and express their relief.

A herald appears and announces that Ajax's brother, Teucer, has arrived from far away and as he was passing through the military camp was insulted by the Argives who called him brother of the madman. Calchas the seer even told Teucer that he might be able to save his brother by keeping him inside his tent that day, as Athena was angry with him for boasting that his strength was sufficient and did not need the help of the gods to win. God's help, he had said, was for the incompetent.

Later, it is reported that Ajax is missing from his tent and eventually is found dead, with his sword thrust in his chest. Teucer talks about the deadly gifts exchanged by the two enemies: Hector was killed and his body was dragged behind a chariot tethered by the belt given to him by Ajax, while Ajax stabbed himself with the sword given to him by Hector.

While Tecmessa and Teucer lament, Menelaus enters the stage and orders that Ajax should remain unburied for plotting against his soldiers. This angers Teucer, an argument follows and Menelaus departs. Agamemnon enters and after calling Teucer the son of a slave, tells him he has no right to object to the orders of his superiors. Teucer reminds him of the many times Ajax had put his life in danger for them and returns the insult about his mother by calling Agamemnon's mother a fornicator. The situation is relieved by the intervention of Odysseus, who praises the bravery of the dead Ajax and persuades the leader to allow his burial. Teucer thanks him and says that while Ajax was alive he was Odysseus' worst enemy within the Greek camp, but now that he is dead he has bestowed on him this great honour. The tragedy ends with the burial of Ajax.

ALCESTIS
(EURIPIDES)

In Thessaly, Apollo comes out of the palace of Admetus. Although a god, he has come to work in the palace of a mortal as part of Zeus' punishment for a murder he had committed. Admetus had been just and respectful towards him and in turn, Apollo had persuaded the deities of fate to make arrangements for Admetus to avoid death if someone else agreed to die in his place. When his time came to die Admetus tried to find someone to take his place. From those he asked, including his parents, the only one who accepted was his wife Alcestis.

When the time comes and Death arrives to take Alcestis, Admetus holds her in his hands. On his way out, Apollo meets Death and asks him not to take her yet but to wait until she grows old. When Death refuses, Apollo foretells that a man who will come to stay in the palace as a guest will take Alcestis from Death's hands.

The chorus appears, composed of Pherrae elders from the city. They speak with respect about Alcestis and wonder if the queen is already dead. A servant comes out of the palace and informs them that the queen is about to die.

Alcestis goes in front of Hestia, the goddess of family life, and beseeches her to take care of her children who are to be left motherless. Then she visits all of the palace's altars and prays as she bids the crying slaves farewell.

Alcestis comes out supported by Admetus who starts weeping, saying that if Alcestis dies he will also perish. She reminds him that this has been her decision. The only thing she asks him is not to give their two children a stepmother inferior to her. After much wailing and a series of promises by Admetus that he will never even speak to another woman, Alcestis passes away.

Then the demigod Heracles, a friend of Admetus, enters. The king does not reveal to him that Alcestis is dead; instead he tells him that he is mourning because one of the women in the palace has died. In spite of this, Admetus insists that Heracles should be his guest for a few days and they enter the palace.

The ceremony of the burial begins. Pheres, Admetus' father, appears and exalts Alcestis for her sacrifice. This angers Admetus who reminds him that he did not agree to die for his son. Pheres responds that it was his right to save his own life and that in the same way Admetus values his life, so does he. He goes as far as to argue that Alcestis should have never agreed to sacrifice herself and that by accepting her offer, Admetus had effectively killed her.

The servant who had accompanied Heracles in the palace comes out and accuses him of drinking, eating and singing at a time of mourning in the palace. Heracles comes out too and learns from the servant that the woman who had died was the queen, Alcestis. He is angry that he had not been informed earlier and, being the greatest of heroes as well as a demigod, decides to try to save her by wrestling with Death.

Heracles departs and Admetus and the chorus return. Admetus wails and says he now wishes to accompany his wife in Hades and that everyone will call him a coward for agreeing to give up his beloved wife in exchange for his own life. The men of the chorus try to solace him but are interrupted by Heracles, who comes accompanied by a woman covered in a sheet from head to toe. He complains to Admetus about not being told of Alcestis' death and being allowed to enjoy himself at the palace. Then Heracles talks about the reason he has returned: he won the woman next to him at an arrow shooting contest and asks Admetus to let her stay in his palace until he returns from his next labour. Admetus tells him to ask someone else to accommodate the woman because she will remind him of Alcestis, and he is also worried that people may think that he being disrespectful to the memory of his late wife. As he speaks he observes the covered woman and becomes upset when he realises that her body is identical to that of his wife. He asks Heracles to take her away. Heracles insists that he lets her stay and even allows him to touch her. Admetus does so, turning his head the other way. Then Heracles removes the sheet covering the woman, revealing that she is no other than Alcestis herself, whom he had won after wrestling with

Death. He explains that she has to remain mute for three days in order to be purified, as she had been offered to the deities of the underworld. Heracles then departs. Admetus is overjoyed and announces celebrations in the city.

ANDROMACHE
(EURIPIDES)

In Thessaly, near Phthia, Andromache is a supplicant in front of Thetis' temple. She is telling her story as the infamous wife of Hector, the prince of Troy who lost her husband and saw her son Astyanax being thrown off the city walls. She has become a slave in the house of Neoptolemus, the son of Achilles and the killer of Hector. She also informs us that Neoptolemus is married to Hermione, the daughter of Helen and Menelaus, has no children with his wife, but has one son with Andromache. Hermione hates her and believes that Andromache's magic is the reason for her infertility and that she is planning to seize her throne. Hermione wants to kill her now that Neoptolemus is away at Delphi, having travelled there to ask the gods for forgiveness because long ago he had accused god Apollo of his father's murder.

A handmaid comes out of the palace. She reveals to Andromache the plan of Hermione and Menelaus to kill her son. The chorus of Phthian women appears and they express their compassion to Andromache.

Hermione steps out of the palace and accuses Andromache of not only sleeping with her husband, but also having a child with him. She orders her to restrict her actions to slave duties alone from then onwards. Andromache replies that she is not responsible for any of the things she is being accused of and Hermione has only herself to blame for her behaviour and for treating Neoptolemus as if he was inferior to her. Hermione threatens that before Neoptolemus is back she will find a way to kill her.

Menelaus comes out of the palace pulling a tied-up boy who begs for his life. Menelaus threatens that, if Andromache does not leave the temple where she is under the protection of the goddess, they will kill her son instead. Andromache replies that if this is the case they will have to face her son's father, and predicts that Neoptolemus will force Hermione out of the palace. Eventually she agrees to leave the temple and when she does so she is arrested by Menelaus' men. Menelaus then tells her that he has been deceived and that he lied when he told her that her child would be spared death, this will be Hermione's decision. They all enter the palace.

Menelaus appears again with his men. They drag in Andromache and her son, tied to one another. Then old Peleus comes in, Neoptolemus' grandfather and requests their release. He gives a depreciatory speech about Menelaus saying that he knew that his wife Helen was unfaithful yet he left her alone with Paris, who took her from him. After that, instead of forgetting about her he declared a war in order to bring her back and by doing so he was responsible for the deaths of so many young men. To Peleus he is also responsible for the death of his son Achilles, who died in the war. He believes he was right to advise his grandson not to marry the daughter of a dishonest mother. Peleus finally orders Menelaus to take Hermione with him and leave the palace. Menelaus accuses Peleus that while his son Achilles had been killed by Paris, a relative of Andromache, he is now on her side. Besides, would he like the possibility of the throne being given to the son of a barbaric woman in the event that there is no other heir?

The head of the chorus attempts to reconcile the two men. Peleus gets angry and threatens that if Menelaus and his barren daughter do not leave the palace he will have her dragged by her hair and driven away. He then proceeds to untie Andromache and her child. Menelaus departs in fear of the consequences and announces that he will no longer occupy himself with the issue of Andromache and that his prime duty now is to deal with a group of rebels near Sparta. When he has dealt with them he will return to settle the issue with his son-in-law. Peleus takes Andromache and the child with him and leaves. When Hermione hears of their departure she becomes exasperated, pulling her hair, crying and attempting to hurt herself with a sword. She fears how her husband will react when he finds out what has happened.

Orestes arrives and Hermione asks him to take her away to save her. He reminds her that initially she was promised to him, but afterwards her father promised to give her as a wife to Neoptolemus if he returned victorious from the Trojan War. When the war was over, Orestes asked Neoptolemus for her hand, but he was rejected and insulted. Orestes promises to Hermione that he will take her to her father and tells her not to be afraid, as he has a plan for the assassination of her husband. He then leaves with her.

Peleus comes back and learns of the departure of Hermione with Orestes and the plans of Orestes to kill Neoptolemus. Immediately, a herald appears and announces that Neoptolemus is dead. He narrates how Orestes had spread the rumour in Delphi that Neoptolemus was planning on stealing the treasures from the temple. When the locals saw Neoptolemus entering the temple to worship, they attacked him. He resisted with bravery and would have won if Apollo was not on his opponents' side. The god had not forgotten his old anger, even though Neoptolemus had gone to his temple to ask for his forgiveness. His entourage picked up his body and brought it back to be mourned and buried by Peleus.

During the mourning the goddess Thetis, the wife of the mortal Peleus and mother of Achilles, appears. She orders Peleus to take the body back to Apollo's temple and bury it there, as a form of reproach against Apollo and Orestes. Then, the goddess says, Peleus should send Andromache to Molossoi for her to become the legal wife of Helenus and their heir the king of Molossoi, so that their family would not perish along with the Trojan people. Finally, Peleus would be made immortal and taken to the palaces of Nereus, deep under the sea. Peleus announces that he will obey Thetis' commands. Along with the chorus, they take the body and enter the palace.

ANTIGONE
(SOPHOCLES)

Outside Creon's palace in Thebes, Antigone and her sister Ismene are arguing about the royal order of their uncle, king Creon, concerning the burial of their two brothers. Eteocles was the king of Thebes and his brother Polynices, who was in exile, organised a military campaign against him to seize the Thebean throne[1]. During the battle both brothers were killed. As Polynices was the one who initiated the attack against his home city, Creon ordered for his body to be dragged out of the city and to be left unburied, to be eaten by the vultures. The body of Eteocles on the other hand was to be buried with honours. Anyone who disobeyed this order would be sentenced to death.

Antigone tells Ismene that she will not abandon her brother Polynices and that she will bury him, even if this act costs her her life. She asks for her help but Ismene argues that

---

1 According to the myth, they had made an agreement to share the throne by taking turns to reign for a year each and then give the throne to the other. However, when the turn of Polynices came, Eteocles refused to hand him the throne. In this version of the story, Polynices is mentioned as being exiled.

they will both suffer the worst if they act against the king's will. Besides, it is not natural for women to rise up against men. Antigone insists, saying that she would rather have the approval of the dead as she will eventually be amongst them forever.

A chorus of Theban elders enters the stage. They narrate the events of the struggle between Eteocles and Polynices which led to their death. Then they announce the entrance of Creon on the stage. Creon explains that he is legitimately the king, being the closest relative of Oedipus, the dead brothers' father. He states that his decision regarding the bodies of the brothers was fair and selects guards to watch over the body of Polynices.

After a while a fearful guard appears and announces that somebody attempted to bury Polynices' body and then disappeared, and none of the guards saw who it was. Creon demands the discovery and immediate arrest of the mysterious person, or else the guards would receive the death penalty; as to him it was evident that they had been bribed.

The same guard reappears carrying Antigone, who was arrested as she was burying Polynices. He stresses the fact that she did not resist her arrest. Antigone defends her actions; she had disobeyed the order of a mortal person that contradicts the unwritten laws of the gods. Creon adopts a hard line even though Antigone is his sister Jocasta's daughter and also engaged to his son, Haemon. He will put to death both her and Ismene, because he believes that Ismene also played a role in the burial. He orders the guards to bring her in, whilst he talks with Antigone. Ismene appears and supports her sister, saying that she also contributed to the burial. Antigone contradicts her using harsh words.

Haemon comes in and tries to persuade his father to reconsider his decision regarding Antigone's punishment. Creon insists, stressing that a ruler must keep his word. The young man uses several arguments to change his mind and says that the people of Thebes are against this decision but Creon remains resolute. Angered by the hardness of his father, Haemon departs, announcing that Creon will never see him again.

After Haemon's intervention, Creon alters his decision. He declares Ismene not guilty, accepting the fact that she had not taken part in the burial. For Antigone he orders her incarceration for life in an underground room in a desolate place with minimal food.

The chorus declares their compassion for Antigone who in her wailing says that being unmarried she will effectively be married to Death, living far away both from the dead and the living, paying for the crimes of her lineage.

Creon returns on the stage; the time has come to take Antigone to her prison. She insists that she righteously honoured her brother. Had her husband or child died, she could marry again or bear more children, but as her parents were dead her brother could never be replaced. She is punished to descend to the abode of the dead for keeping her respect towards the gods.

The old blind seer Teiresias appears. He argues with

Creon, saying that his decision is wrong. Creon attacks him without respect, but Teiresias insists, foreseeing that if he does not change his decision, Creon will see one of his own offspring dead. At long last the king is persuaded to change his mind and personally goes to free Antigone.

A herald enters the stage announcing that Haemon has committed suicide. The herald had accompanied Creon to the place where the body of Polynices lay half-eaten by dogs and buried it with him. When approaching Antigone's cell, Haemon was heard wailing inside. Upon entering the room, they saw Antigone hanged by her belt and Haemon weeping over her body. When he saw the king, Haemon raised his sword and attacked him. The king stepped backwards, then Haemon turned the sword towards himself and, hugging Antigone with his other hand, killed himself. Eurydice, Haemon's mother and the wife of Creon, who was listening to the herald, leaves and enters the palace. Creon approaches holding Haemon in his arms, mourning and blaming himself for his death. The herald, who had entered the palace, comes out. He narrates that inside the palace, cursing Creon, Eurydice had committed suicide by thrusting a knife under her liver. Creon wails and wishes to die.

The chorus closes the tragedy by saying that prudence is the main element of happiness and that one must never show disrespect towards the Divine.

THE BACCHAE
(EURIPIDES)

The god Dionysus (or Bacchus) is in Thebes in the form of a handsome young man. He is standing in front of the palace of Pentheus, Cadmus' grandson. After announcing that he is the son of Zeus and Semele, Cadmus' daughter, he narrates what happened to his mother when she was pregnant with him as a result of Zeus' jealous wife, Hera, who trapped her so that she was hit by Zeus' thunder. He adds that he punished his mother's sisters, Agave and Ino, for spreading the rumour that he was the fruit of his mother's adultery with a mortal and not the son of Zeus, the father of the gods. Dionysus made them lose their minds and live on the mountains, where they participated in his rituals. He says that it is now Pentheus' turn to be punished, as like the others he too refuses to accept his divine nature.

He calls his female followers, the Bacchae, also known as Maenads, who make up the chorus of the tragedy. They look strange: their hair is untidy and instead of clothes they are dressed in deer skins. He orders them to play their Phrygian drums around the palace so that everyone notices them and departs for Mount Cithaeron to participate in the Bacchic rituals taking place there.

The Bacchae speak of the thunder with which Zeus unknowingly hit Semele and then took her foetus and inserted it inside his thigh, while keeping it a secret from Hera. Nine months later Dionysus was born.

Teiresias the seer, appears; he is old and blind. He is dressed in deer skins and is wearing an ivy crown on his head. He meets Cadmus who is dressed in a similar way and they prepare to organise Bacchic dances to worship Dionysus.

Pentheus appears, angry with the new customs. He announces that any woman from Thebes going to the mountain to participate in Dionysian rituals will be arrested, even if she is his own mother. He tells his grandfather, Cadmus, to take off the ridiculous ivy from his head and accuses Teiresias of supporting the god as an attraction with the sole purpose of making money through requests for prophecies. As a reply, Teiresias confirms the divine nature of Dionysus, but Pentheus is not convinced and orders the arrest and execution of the handsome young man who excites women.

Two servants arrest Dionysus, tie him, and bring him to Pentheus. They say that he did not resist, but the doors of the prisons in which they had imprisoned the Bacchae opened by themselves and the women, freed, took to the near meadows and started dancing as if they were crazy.

Pentheus questions Dionysus about the rituals, but the god does not give away any details. Pentheus orders his imprisonment. Dionysus causes Pentheus to hallucinate which results in him tying up a bull thinking it is Dionysus. The god also causes an earthquake and sets fire to Semele's tomb nearby, so that Pentheus thinks that his palace is burning. An upset Pentheus searches for Dionysus, who tells him that a god set him free.

A herald appears; he announces that he comes from Cithaeron, from where he barely managed to escape. When he attempted to arrest Agave, the women got so angry that nobody could control them. From the miracles he had witnessed on the mountain, the herald was persuaded that Dionysus was indeed a god and asks Pentheus to accept his divine nature. Pentheus refuses and decides to arrest the Bacchae with the help of the army. In order to ridicule and banish him, Dionysus suggests to Pentheus to view the rituals. He will lead him there himself; all Pentheus has to do is dress as a woman and pretend to be a member of Bacchae so that he is not killed for being a man. Pentheus gets dressed in women's clothes and walking through Thebes, they depart for the mountains.

A herald comes with the news that while on Cithaeron, Pentheus asked to be taken to a high spot so he can observe the Bacchae from above. Dionysus bent a tall tree and placed Pentheus on it while shouting "This is the man who ridicules us. Punish him!". Pentheus' mother, Agave, being in an ecstatic state as part of the female crowd did not recognise her son; in her eyes he appeared as a lion which must be killed. Pentheus took his dress off, but in vain. With the help of the Bacchae, his mother cut him into pieces, decapitating him and impaling his head on a pole.

Returning to Thebes with the pole in hand, Agave comes to her senses and realises what she has done. Desperation and horror overtake her. Cadmus tells her that with much difficulty he managed to collect the pieces of her son's cut up body and has already taken them to the palace.

Agave and Cadmus are mourning. Dionysus appears and explains that everything happened as a result of their failure to acknowledge him and worship him as a god. He orders that Cadmus, Agave and her sisters should all be exiled from the city.

The tragedy ends with the departure of Cadmus and Agave, with the latter asking to go to far away places from where she would never see Mount Cithaeron again.

HECABE
(EURIPIDES)

In Thrace, in front of the tents housing Trojan women captured by the Achaeans, appears the ghost of Polydorus, the son of one of the women, queen Hecabe. The ghost explains how his father Priam, fearing the fall of Troy, had sent him to Polymestor, the king of Thrace, to ensure his safety. The king was attending him well but after Troy fell to the Greek army Polymestor killed him so that he could keep the gold with which Priam had sent him to Thrace. The body of Polydorus was thrown in the sea and ended up on these shores, having asked the gods to direct his body to his mother in order for her to bury it. He also says that his mother will see his sister, Polyxene, dead. Polyxene is to be sacrificed by the Achaeans following Achilles' ghost's request that she would be slaughtered on his grave as a sacrifice. As Polydorus narrates the above, his mother Hecabe comes slowly out of her tent. She describes the terrible dreams she had about Polydorus and Polyxene.

The chorus of the enslaved Trojan women announces to Hecabe that the Achaeans have decided to sacrifice her daughter. As Hecabe wails, Polyxene comes out of a tent and hears the news and they start lamenting together. Polyxene says that she is only lamenting for her mother, because she will have no one to look after her in her old age. Polyxene, as events have turned out, prefers death.

Odysseus enters the stage. Hecabe, reminding him that she once saved his life, asks him to mediate so that her child is spared. They could sacrifice bulls or even Helen in her place, Helen being the original cause of all evils. Odysseus replies that Achilles has died for Greece and so he has the right to be honoured as he wishes. Polyxene intervenes and says that she is not afraid, since death is better than the life she has been condemned to. The chorus admires her bravery. Hecabe insists, suggesting to the Achaeans to accept her as a sacrifice but in vain. When Odysseus refuses, she says that if this is the case she will follow her daughter to death. She embraces Polyxene tightly. Odysseus separates the two women and Hecabe starts mourning.

After a while, the herald Talthybius arrives, sent by Agamemnon to tell Hecabe that the sacrifice is complete and she can proceed with the burial of her daughter. Hecabe orders the Argives that nobody is to touch the body of Polyxene and starts the preparations for her burial. She sends her handmaid to fill a jug with sea water for Polyxene's last bath.

The handmaid returns carrying a heavy load, which she puts down. She reveals to Hecabe that she is bringing the body of her dead son, which she found on the seashore. Hecabe, aware of the gold he was sent to Thrace with, suspects

Polymestor at once. As she starts cursing him, Agamemnon arrives to find out what has happened and why Hecabe has not yet been to collect her daughter's body.

He sees Hecabe wailing in front of a corpse and asks who the dead man is. Before answering, the queen kneels as a suppliant in front of him. She tells him the story of her son and asks him to help her punish the murderer as he deserves, or at least to allow her to settle the matter herself. She asks him not to stop her handmaid from calling Polymestor and his two children and to delay her daughter's burial. In this task she will be assisted by the captured Trojan women, who have always been faithful to her.

Polymestor arrives with his two sons and hypocritically expresses his deep sorrow for Polyxene's death. Hecabe asks him to let his followers depart because she has a secret to tell him. Polymestor orders them to leave and Hecabe asks him about Polydorus. He assures her that all is well with him, thus confirming her suspicions. Hecabe tells him that all of king Priam's gold is buried underground at a place only she knows. She will reveal it to him, so that he, in turn, can reveal it to her son. She has also brought gold from Troy and wants him to look after it for her.

Hecabe then enters the tent with Polymestor and his sons. Screams are heard as her servants blind Polymestor and kill his sons. The women of the chorus leave the tent carrying the bodies of the sons. The blinded Polymestor also comes out, asking for help.

Agamemnon appears and Polymestor asks for Hecabe to

be punished. He defends himself by saying that the reason he killed Polydorus was that in the future he could rebuild Troy and the Greeks would go out to conquer it again, and by doing so they would loot his own country, Thrace, once again as happened the first time. He also claims he did it to protect Agamemnon from possible future enemies. Hecabe intervenes, arguing that the sole reason for the murder was the gold; if Polymestor was a friend of the Achaeans he should have given the gold to them, as he knows they are having a very hard time away from their homes. She then asks Agamemnon not to help him.

When Polymestor notices that Agamemnon is indeed unwilling to help, he starts cursing and mentions that Dionysus has given an oracle that Hecabe will die by falling off a ship's mast and then take the form of a dog. Not only she, but also her daughter Cassandra will suffer a violent death. Polymestor also tells Agamemnon that death awaits him by the hands of his wife, Clytemnestra. This angers Agamemnon who orders his exile on a desert island as a punishment. He allows Hecabe to bury her dead children and Hecabe, together with the other women, take the corpse of Polydorus and depart.

HELEN
(EURIPIDES)

Helen is in Egypt, suppliant in front of the tomb of king Proteus. In her monologue, she explains that she is unfairly blamed as the cause of the Trojan War. She was not Paris' prize for judging the beauty contest between the three goddesses, Hera, Aphrodite and Athena – Paris took with him an effigy of Helen. Helen herself was wrapped in a cloud by Hermes and was brought to the honest king Proteus, so that after the war was over she would be given back to her husband Menelaus. But when Proteus died, his son Theoclymenus became king and persistently asked her to become his wife. So she is now begging the dead king to continue to guard her honour.

Teucer, Ajax's stepbrother appears on the stage and is surprised how much the woman resembles the loathsome Helen of Troy. Helen assures him that she is not the woman hated all over the country and Teucer, relieved, answers her questions. He tells her that the war had ended seven years ago. Menelaus was lost and considered dead. Leda, Helen's mother, hanged herself reportedly out of shame for her daughter's actions, and that rumour had it that Helen's brothers, Castor and Polydeuces, (Dioscouroi), were either killed or transformed into stars by the gods.

Teucer reveals to Helen that the reason he had come to Egypt was to receive an oracle by Theonoe, the king's sister, for the best way to travel to Cyprus. Helen warns Teucer to leave and tells him that the new king will kill him as soon as he sees him, as he does with all Greek people who arrive in his country. Teucer thanks her and leaves.

The chorus arrives, consisting of a group of Greek female slaves. A weeping Helen announces the horrible news. Her destiny has imposed the burden of a whole war on her, yet she bears no responsibility for it. She thinks that if she returns to her home city she will be exiled, therefore the best solution for her is death. The chorus feels compassionate towards her. Helen decides to ask Theonoe for an oracle in order to learn about her husband. If he is indeed dead then she will take her own life. All the women enter the palace for the oracle and the stage empties.

Menelaus appears, announcing that his ship was wrecked. He was saved along with Helen and just a few sailors. He had hidden Helen inside a cave to be guarded by his companions and went wandering in search of food. An old woman appears and advises him to leave; in this country, she says, they kill Greeks. The reason for such hatred is a Spartan woman, Helen, Zeus' daughter, who came here before the Trojan War. The old woman enters the palace and leaves Menelaus puzzled by what she has just said.

Menelaus walks towards the tomb of Proteus as the

chorus emerges again. They say that according to the oracle, Menelaus is alive but lost at sea. Then Helen appears, full of hope. She watches the man standing in front of the tomb and at first does not recognise him. Then she tells him how much he reminds her of Menelaus and he tells her how much she resembles his wife Helen. Helen joyfully informs him that she is Helen but Menelaus does not believe her. However a herald arrives and confirms that his wife flew, leaving the cave empty, and declares that she was not the true Helen but an effigy, and that the Achaeans had been fooled. Helen's reputation was damaged without her being at fault.

A scene where the couple declare their undying love for one another follows. After 17 whole years, ten years of war and another seven away from home, Menelaus and Helen are still in love. They talk about what happened during these years, and blame Paris, but more so the gods. Theonoe appears and declares that she is facing a dilemma: should she tell Theoclymenus the truth about who Menelaus really is or not? Helen tells her that Theonoe's father, an honest man, would have liked to give Menelaus what belonged to him and asks her to keep his identity secret. Menelaus declares that if necessary he will duel with the king and if defeated he will commit suicide, taking Helen to the grave with him. Theonoe promises to help them by not telling a word to her brother. Then Helen proposes a rescue plan.

Theoclymenus appears and Helen puts her plan at work. She tells him, pointing to Menelaus, that the castaway brought her the bad news that her husband had died at sea and the effigy responsible for the Trojan War disappeared in the air. She will now become his wife but first she asks him for a ship, sacrifices, fruits and weapons in order to honour her dead husband the way he deserves, by dispersing the items into the sea, as is the custom in her homeland when a warrior drowns. Theoclymenus does not believe her but she argues that if she was lying, Theonoe, who is a seeress, would know. Hearing this the king changes his mind and gives her a ship and rowers to honour the dead Menelaus in the open sea, as she should. Helen and Menelaus board the ship and leave.

After their escape, a herald comes and narrates the end of the story. A group of sailors from Menelaus' fleet had secretly entered the boat, killed the rowers and threw their bodies in the sea. Now they have all departed for Greece. Theoclymenus decides to punish Theonoe with the death penalty because she was aware of the truth about Menelaus and did not reveal it.

Then the Dioscouroi appear, who tell the king that they will not allow him to touch Theonoe, since they are gods and consider the escape of their sister Helen an act of justice. Theoclymenus is persuaded and promises not to touch Theonoe, adding that their sister was an honest woman, full of virtue and prudence.

SEVEN AGAINST THEBES
(AESCHYLUS)

Eteocles[1], the king of Thebes, addresses the people of the city in front of the Cadmeian Citadel and tries to encourage them to face the invading army.

A herald brings the news that the Argive army is outside the city walls. He says that the enemy's plan of attack had been decided. Each of their seven leaders would attack each of the seven gates of the city, taking a ballot to decide who would go to which gate. The herald asks Eteocles to choose the best of his military leaders to face them.

A chorus of Thebaean virgins comes in. They are lamenting, having seen the Argive army in front of their city. Waves of men and many horses are spreading fear; terrified,

---

1 Oedipus' sons, Eteocles and Polynices were carrying their father's curse, uttered when he learned that they were the fruit of his incest with his mother. He had cursed them to divide their inheritance "by the sword". So Polynices had orchestrated a military campaign against his brother, who had previously exiled him. The army following him was the army of Argos, since he had married the daughter of their king.

the virgins seek help from the gods.

Hearing their cries, Eteocles returns and tries to calm them down. He uses harsh words and says they must be calm in order to encourage the soldiers, instead of spreading fear with their words. Despite the warning, the chorus girls do not change their tune; they are afraid of death, captivity and the destruction of their city.

Another herald announces that the seven leaders of the enemy have deployed their forces against the seven gates of the walls. He describes the warlike and untamed character of the seven warriors and their shields, upon which terrible images are carved to inspire fear to the opponent. Eteocles chooses the Thebaeans who will guard the gates against the attacks, describing each of them with flattering words. The last gate will be guarded by him, against his brother, Polynices.

A dialog between Eteocles and the chorus follows. The chorus tries to dissuade him from going up against his brother this way but the efforts of the virgins are in vain and Eteocles is adamant. In this conversation before the battle, Oedipus' curse is mentioned. This is what the evil pursuing the two brothers is attributed to, along with Apollo's oracle given to Oedipus' father Laius. According to this if he was to be saved he should not have children; if he did, his descendants would be cursed. The chorus reminds Eteocles of Oedipus' curse to his sons but despite this the king leaves for battle.

A herald brings news from the battle in progress. At the six of the seven gates, the enemies of the city were faced with courage by the Thebaean warriors and were defeated. At the seventh gate –where the fight between the two brothers would decide the final outcome of the war– both were killed, each by the other's sword, and their dead bodies now lay on the ground next to one another.

The chorus, divided in two semi-choruses, laments for the loss of the brothers, stressing the curse they were unable to escape. Together with the chorus, their sister Antigone participates in the mourning.

Another herald appears, announcing that the city elders decided that Eteocles, being a defender of the city, will be buried with royal honours, while Polynices will remain unburied, for his intention was to destroy the city.

Antigone reacts to this decision, claiming that the elders are unjustly discriminating against Polynices. She will bury Polynices, even if her action has repercussions.

The tragedy ends with the chorus of the virgins remaining divided into two semi-choruses. The one half agrees with the decision to leave Polynices unburied, while the other half supports Antigone. One group of girls promise that they will follow Antigone to the burial and mourning of Polynices, while the other will participate in the ceremony for the funeral of Eteocles.

EUMENIDES – ORESTEIA, PART III
(AESCHYLUS)

The stage hosts the temple of Apollo in Delphi, where Orestes stands a suppliant with blood dripping from his hands. Around him, the Furies form the chorus of the tragedy. The creatures, horrible in their appearance, clad in black with black pus running out of their eyes, are asleep.

Apollo appears. He speaks to Orestes, assuring him that he wants to assist him. He advises him to leave immediately, because as soon as the Furies wake up, they will chase him. Orestes must travel to Athens as a suppliant of goddess Athena, where he will be judged for the murder of his mother, Clytemnestra. Apollo will help him by saying that he was the one who ordered him to kill her and for this reason Orestes is not to be blamed.

The ghost of Clytemnestra appears saying she is wandering in Hades dishonoured because of the murder she had committed. She complains that although she was the victim of her own family, no god had supported her despite her always worshipping them with sacrifices. She wakes the goddesses of the Underworld and urges them to hurry in order to catch Orestes and blow on him the air of death.

The Furies wake up and accuse Apollo of disrespecting them by supporting Orestes' matricide. He should not be behaving this way when he is one of the newest Olympian gods, while they are amongst the oldest deities. He was sly when helping him to escape their punishment. Apollo orders the Furies to get out of his temple immediately, accusing them of not pursuing all killers with the same zest, as they seem to forget that Clytemnestra had also murdered her husband. They respond that killing a blood relative is always different and insist on punishing Orestes for the murder he committed. Apollo replies that they are chasing him in vain, as the final decision rests with Athena.

In the next scene we are taken to Athens, where Orestes is suppliant in Athena's temple. The chorus of Furies arrives. Seeing Orestes angers them and they declare that nothing will rescue him from their hands. Orestes argues that his crime has already been cleansed as he has performed sacrifices at Apollo's altar, but to no avail. The Furies insist that they will never leave him alone. They operate completely independently from the Olympian gods and they have to be respected by anyone who has committed a crime, dead or alive.

The goddess Athena appears and wants to know the situation of the suppliant. The Furies speak first by introducing themselves: they are the daughters of Night and Zeus and are chasing the matricide. Orestes announces to Athena that he is the son of Agamemnon. He narrates his story to her and stresses that god Apollo had prophesied that he would suffer terribly if he did not kill those responsible for his father's murder. The Furies insist that the burden of a crime that is impossible to cleanse is on Orestes' shoulders. Athena says that, in order to decide who is right, she needs the help of a court with judges under oath. The Furies object: this way, they argue, new ethics are introduced and they fear that certain laws which were under their sole jurisdiction will not be respected. They add that if Orestes gets away with the murder of his own mother then every other murderer will also be set free, and "in some cases, it is a good thing for fear to stay as a guard of the mind". The view of the Furies, however, is ignored by Athena who summons the court.

Orestes admits he committed the murder, yet insists that he is not guilty. His mother was the one who was guilty of murder. Apollo comes in as a witness for the defense saying that the oracle he gave to Orestes that he should take revenge for his father's death was given under orders by Zeus. The murder of the father is more serious a crime than that of the mother, whose role is merely to bear the child in her womb, nursing the male's seed. The Furies insist on their position regarding Orestes' guilt and threaten that if the court's decision violates their rights and jurisdiction, they will take their revenge by punishing Athena's country.

After that the judges take a vote, with Athena voting last. She votes for Orestes' innocence, saying that as she herself was not born by a woman she prefers men and will therefore support Orestes for defending his father's honour. The number of votes is equal for both sides, which is considered an acquittal for Orestes who leaves for his country free. The Furies are mad with anger and shout threats against the city that set the killer free, but Athena sooths them by stressing that their position was not undermined, as the number of votes cast for each side was equal, even if the decision turned out to be against their will. She promises that they will have altars built in their honour and enjoy respect in her city.

Athena manages to propitiate the Furies by turning them to Eumenidae (which is also the title of this tragedy), which means that the deities now have a good disposition towards the city. On this positive note the tragedy ends.

ELECTRA
(EURIPIDES)

A poorly dressed man leaves a small hut outside the city of Argos. He is Electra's husband, a farmer, and speaks about the event of the murder of her father, Agamemnon. Agamemnon was killed by her mother, Clytemnestra, who acted together with Aegisthus, Clytemnestra's new husband and king. From their children, Orestes was helped to escape by his pedagogue, while Electra, who Aegisthus was planning on killing, was saved by her mother. Eventually, Aegisthus issued a proclamation for Orestes and married Electra to the farmer. From his words we learn that, as he is not worthy of her, their marriage is fake.

Electra appears, looking scruffy and dressed in rags. From her attitude when she meets her husband it is evident that they share mutual compassion and respect. Electra tells him that she is going to bring water and leaves.

Orestes enters with his friend Pylades. Orestes has returned secretly to his home city in order to take revenge for his father's murder. Seeing Electra coming, he mistakes her for a slave and hides. Electra speaks of her misery and of her waiting for revenge for her father's murder. The chorus consisting of Argive women arrives and they inform her that major celebrations will be taking place and that all girls are to go to Hera's temple. Electra says that she is not interested and that mourning is the only thing she wants to do. The chorus advises her to put things behind her and to take better care of herself, but Electra is not persuaded.

Orestes and Pylades approach her and tell her they are bringing news from her brother. Electra gets excited and tells them about her misery: her wedding which was arranged so that any child arising from it would not have rights to the throne, being a farmer's child, and that Aegisthus profanes their father's tomb and is cursing Orestes. She asks them for a favour: to tell her brother everything she just told them, for it would be a shame on him not to kill Aegisthus.

Electra's husband appears and invites the strangers in their humble house. They call the old pedagogue to hear the news and as he comes in he says that there are signs at Agamemnon's tomb to indicate that Orestes may have secretly already arrived in the city. At this point, the two friends leave the hut. The pedagogue recognises Orestes from an old mark on his eyebrow and with great joy brother and sister recognise each other. They agree that the time for revenge has come and devise a plan; Orestes will meet Aegisthus, while the old educator would go to announce to their mother that Electra has just given birth and ask her to come to see her. Electra enters the hut.

A herald arrives and describes the murder of Aegisthus in the fields, where he was offering sacrifices. When he saw two strangers, he invited them to participate. While Aegisthus was examining the sacrificed animal, Orestes killed him using the knife Aegisthus had given him to kill the animal. The servants rushed to hit them, but when they recognised Orestes they put a wreath on his head and started shouting with joy.

Orestes and Pylades appear on stage together with attendants who carry the corpse of Aegisthus. They offer it as a present to Electra, who accepts it with words full of hatred and bitterness both for him and her mother. She tells the servants to hide the corpse in the hut, so that her mother does not see it when she comes in; then Orestes will kill her, too. Orestes is hesitating about this murder and doubts Apollo's oracle that urges him to kill his own mother. However, Electra exhorts him and he finally agrees.

Clytemnestra comes to see her daughter, believing that she has just given birth. The two talk and Clytemnestra does not accept responsibility for Agamemnon's murder. She says he was to be blamed for deceiving and sacrificing her daughter Iphigenia, and then for returning from the war bringing with him a new lover and neglecting her. Electra, however, accuses her that her hatred for Agamemnon was there before the sacrifice and that she did not only murder him, but also allowed Aegisthus to take over their palace. Clytemnestra shows a conciliatory attitude, telling her daughter that she knows she had always loved her father more than she loved her but she is not holding that against her and she does not feel happy about her deeds either. They argue and Electra invites her mother to enter the hut. Seeing Orestes with a sword in his hand, she realises she has fallen in a trap. She bares her chest and kneels, begging Orestes to spare her. Orestes lets the sword fall from his hand, but then covering his eyes with his cloak, cuts his mother's throat, aided by Electra.

All three, Pylades, Orestes and Electra leave the hut with blood dripping from their hands and clothes. The bodies of Clytemnestra and Aegisthus are presented to the audience. Orestes feels guilty for his act and starts wondering in fear how he will be able to withstand this guilt. Electra is also suffering, calling her mother "beloved and hated at the same time". She says that no man would ever accept her as his wife when she, too, is indirectly a murderer.

The Dioscouroi (Castor and Polydeuces, Helen and Clytemnestra's brothers) appear as Deus ex machina. They advise Orestes to travel to Athens where the gods will judge him for his crime. They predict that the judgment will result in a tie of votes and subsequently in his acquittal. Orestes will give Electra as a wife to Pylades. Her current husband will be offered gifts and will be sent to live in Phocis.

ELECTRA
(SOPHOCLES)

In front of the palace of the Atreides, in Mycenae, Orestes is talking with his friend Pylades and his pedagogue. The pedagogue tells Orestes that this is the place where he had taken him from his sister Electra's hands, still a little boy, when his father Agamemnon was murdered. It is revealed that Orestes has returned to the city in order to take revenge for the murder of his father and has a plan based on an oracle given to him by god Apollo. Apollo had ordered him to murder those responsible by deceiving them. Orestes decides that the pedagogue should make an announcement in the palace that he brings news of Orestes' death in a chariot racing accident. They exit to pour libations on Agamemnon's tomb.

A woman can be heard wailing. It is Electra, who begs the gods to punish her father's killers and bring her brother back. The chorus, a group of Argive maidens, comes in and advises Electra to stop wailing. Electra ignores them and keeps crying, while the chorus insists that it is not advisable to turn against those in power. Electra replies that she hates her mother, Clytemnestra, her relentless enemy who every month celebrates with dances and sacrifices the day she murdered her husband. Electra also hates Aegisthus, who sits on her father's throne and offers libations on the palace's hearth, the very place they had killed Agamemnon. Her mother offends her for lamenting, also blaming her for taking Orestes from her hands in order to save him.

Chrysothemis, Electra's sister, leaves the palace. She advises her to stop behaving the way she is and obey those in power. Electra, however, complains to her; not only she is not helping her to take revenge but on the contrary, she is being submissive because she does not want to lose her comforts and honours. The chorus exhorts the sisters to love each other. Chrysothemis reveals that she heard that if Electra does not stop wailing and cursing, Aegisthus will imprison her in an underground jail. Electra says that perhaps this would be a good solution as she would then stop witnessing what is going on.

Chrysothemis, changing the subject, tells Electra that their mother has sent her to offer libations on their father's tomb, after a strange dream had frightened her. She dreamt that Agamemnon was alive and that he dug his sceptre into the ground, whereupon a tall tree sprang, with dense branches and foliage, which covered the whole country. Electra persuades the frightened Chrysothemis to replace the offerings of the murdereress with two of their curls and a belt, so that they will have their dead father on their side when the hour of revenge comes.

Clytemnestra appears. She argues with Electra and tells

her to stop complaining. She accepts with audacity that she committed the murder and says that she does not feel any guilt, as what happened was the decision of Dike, the goddess of justice. Electra refuses to accept her mother's excuses and Clytemnestra threatens her by saying that as soon as Aegisthus returns she will be punished for her attitude. The queen asks her to stop talking so that she can make a sacrifice to Apollo, to whom she prays for the continuous enjoyment of wealth for her and Aegisthus. Implicitly, she furtively asks for the demise of Orestes.

The pedagogue arrives bringing the news about Orestes' death. Listening to him, Electra starts wailing more intensely. The chorus comes in and tries to give her some hope, but to no avail. Chrysothemis also appears. She believes that Orestes is alive, even somewhere near them; she found cut hair on their father's grave and it cannot be anyone else's. Electra, however, speaks about the newly received information of his death and asks her to help her to take revenge. The younger sister says that being women they are not allowed to do such things. Electra insists that it is their duty to act the way she proposed. Finally Chrysothemis exits with neither of the sisters managing to persuade the other.

The two friends, Orestes and Pylades, appear on stage. They give Electra, who they mistake for a palace slave, the funeral urn that supposedly contains the ashes of Orestes. When Electra starts wailing Orestes recognises her and reveals his true identity to her. Electra is happy and enthusiastic. Orestes tells her to contain her excitement;

only if they are very careful they will succeed in their revenge. She informs him that Aegisthus is absent and that their mother is alone in the palace. The pedagogue participates in the planning. Orestes tells Electra that he is the person to whom she had entrusted him as an infant. Orestes and Pylades enter the palace, where Orestes kills his mother with Electra's encouragement.

After a while, Aegisthus comes in. The two friends inform him about the supposed death of Orestes and Aegisthus is receptive of such happy news. He sees a covered body and uncovers it. This reveals Clytemnestra's corpse and he realises that his time has come.

Orestes leads Aegisthus into the palace where he kills him in the same room where Agamemnon had been murdered, finally taking the revenge that he so longed for. The chorus sings for the children of Atreus who after many adventures were rendered worthy of their freedom.

HERACLIDAE
(EURIPIDES)

In Marathon, near Athens, in front of the temple of Zeus, the children of Heracles, collectively known as Heraclidae, are standing together with Iolaus, their uncle and protector. After their father's death, the king of the Argives, Eurystheus, wants to kill them and they wander in exile from place to place. Wherever they go, heralds are sent to capture them.

Besides Iolaus, who takes care of the boys, Alcmene, their grandmother, has come to take care of the girls. A herald from Eurystheus arrives and attempts to take the children to be stoned in Argos. The chorus of Marathon elders enters the scene.

The herald learns that the ruler of the city is Demophon. When Demophon enters, he informs him that the children are Argives and have been sentenced to death. The herald asks him to hand them over to him, promising that the Argives will offer Demophon their alliance and rich rewards. Otherwise, they will take them with war. The chorus advises that the children's story should also be heard.

Iolaus says that he and the children have been exiled

from Argos and therefore cannot be arrested as Argive citizens. He invokes the right of a foreigner's protection. He reminds them that Heracles was a relative of the king of Athens and mentions that he was the one who took Theseus, Demophon's father, out of Hades, the kingdom of the dead.

The chorus and Demophon are moved, as they are not dealing just with suppliants, but with foreigners who also proved to be their relatives. When the herald hears the Athenians' reaction, he uses the threat of war as a means of pressuring them. Demophon drives him away angrily and starts preparing for war, organising sacrifices to the gods and demanding oracles by the prophets. The foreigners enter the temple as suppliants, praying in favour of the city.

The chorus agrees with Demophon's decision. The king exits and reappears together with his brother, Acamas. They announce that the Athenians are now ready for war and that the army of the Argives has already entered Attica. At the same time, it is revealed that all oracles agree that in order for the war to have a favourable outcome, the sacrifice of a virgin to goddess Demeter is required. However Demophon refuses to sacrifice his or any other Athenian's daughter for the sake of foreign children. If he issued such an order his people would rouse and a civil war would probably follow. He and Iolaus must find another solution. Iolaus proposes to be given to Eurystheus himself to save the children. But Demophon knows that Eurystheus has come for the children, as he is afraid of their vengeance when they come of age, and that Iolaus' proposition would not stop the attack of the Argive army.

Macaria, a daughter of Heracles, gets out of the temple. She learns the news and volunteers to be the one who is sacrificed. The chorus and Iolaus admire her bravery, but Iolaus suggests casting lots amongst the daughters of Heracles. Macaria is not wiling to die by mere chance arguing that if one is willing to die for a purpose, then their death should only be by their own decision. She then leaves.

A servant comes and announces that Hyllus, another of Heracles' sons has arrived with an army and has joined the Athenians. The enemy's army has already approached. Iolaus, despite his old age, decides to take part in combat. The chorus tries to dissuade him, but to no avail.

Before the battle starts, Hyllus asks the Argive leader, king Eurystheus, to duel with him in person instead of resorting to war but Eurystheus, known in mythology as a coward, does not accept. The war begins and the Athenian army wins. Iolaus prays to the gods to make him young again, just for one day. The gods satisfy his wish and, taking Hyllus' chariot, he pursues and arrests Eurystheus.

A slave comes bringing Eurystheus chained. Iolaus offers him as a slave to Alcmene, who, full of hatred, says she will kill him because of everything he has done against her offspring. The chorus objects arguing that there is a law forbidding killing prisoners of war arrested in combat. Eurystheus says that what happened was not his fault: without his consent, goddess Hera, Zeus' wife, filled him with passionate hatred against Heracles for being an illegitimate son of Zeus and

Alcmene and made him hunt him down and torment him. After Heracles' death, he was obliged to hunt down and exterminate his children in order to protect himself from their future vengeance. He also reveals an oracle that said that if he was buried next to Athena's temple, he would protect Athens from the descendants of Heraclidae, who, forgetting the favour they had received, would at some point in the future launch an expedition against Athens. Hearing this, Alcmene, surpassing all her hesitations, finally makes the decision and orders the slaves to kill him and then throw his body to the dogs. The tragedy ends with the cruel death of Eurystheus.

HERAKLES
(EURIPIDES)

I n front of Amphitryon's palace in Thebes there is the altar of Zeus. Around it stands Heracles' whole family: his wife Megara, his mortal stepfather Amphitryon and their three children. Lycus, a descendant of an old king of Thebes, has killed Creon, the previous king and father of Megara and is now threatening to exterminate all of his relatives. Heracles is absent, he has gone to Hades, the Underworld, to accomplish his twelfth and last labour, to take the three-headed monster dog, Cerberus.

The chorus, a group of Thebaean elders, enters. They speak words of compassion towards the family.

Lycus appears and announces that there is no hope for Megara and Amphitryon, because Heracles will not come back from Hades. He calls him a coward, accusing him of always fighting from a distance, using his arrows. Amphitryon defends Heracles passionately. Lycus orders to prepare fires around the altars to burn the father, wife and children. He also threatens the elders, wanting to make clear to everyone that he is now the ruler of the land.

The chorus of elders, talking to Lycus, stresses that they

will never acknowledge him as their king and they will not allow anyone to touch Heracles' children. Megara thanks the elders for their support, but in fear of retaliation asks them to stop defending them. She states that she prefers death than the dishonour of exile. Unconvinced that Heracles will return, she accepts to be put to death by Lycus. Megara asks to be allowed to enter the palace so that she can prepare her children's burial decorations. Lycus agrees and exits.

Megara enters the palace together with Amphitryon who is accusing Zeus, the king of gods and father of Heracles, of abandoning Heracles' sons to their fate, an attitude showing that he is either a god with little sense, or else simply unjust. A glorifying hymn by the chorus follows and the labours of Heracles are narrated, one by one.

Amphitryon appears together with Megara and the children. Megara speaks to them and mourns, while Amphitryon prays to Zeus: if he is to do something to save them, he has to do it immediately. Indeed, Heracles now appears, having returned to Thebes. He learns the news and becomes furious. He orders them to remove the burial decorations: he will soon resolve the situation and punish the culprit.

Amphitryon warns Heracles that by now the king has allies in the city and suggests to him to capture Lycus. He tells Heracles to hide inside the palace and only come out when Lycus comes to take them. Heracles agrees. During their conversation, Heracles informs his mortal father that he had indeed been to Hades and the reason for his delay was that besides Cerberus, he also brought back on earth Theseus, the king of Athens. The stage empties except for the chorus, who once again recites words full of admiration for Heracles.

Lycus and his attendants enter the palace. Soon, his screams are heard and it becomes clear that he is being killed. The chorus can also be heard, triumphantly announcing the death of Lycus and the prevalence of justice.

However even before the elders can finish their hymns about the justice of the gods, two goddesses appear over the palace, Iris and Lyssa (madness). They have come to carry out the will of goddess Hera: they will first drive Heracles mad and then lead him to murder his own children. Lyssa raises her objections; Heracles is not unworthy and shows respect towards the gods. But Iris is adamant and Lyssa gives in. The chorus, full of horror, announces that, exactly as the two goddesses have said Heracles is attacking his children as a maniac.

Amphitryon is heard asking for help. A herald coming out of the palace describes how Heracles, having completely lost his mind, believed that he was on his chariot, running towards Mycenae against Eurystheus. He recognised neither Amphitryon, nor his wife. Eventually, mistaking his children for those of Eurystheus, he was unable to contain his hatred for their father and killed them. The last one he killed together with Megara, using an arrow. As he was ready to kill old Amphitryon, goddess Athena intervened, throwing a heavy stone on his chest. Then Heracles fell into a deep sleep and was tied tightly on a column, out of fear that he would start a new cycle of killings when he woke up. Upon finishing narrating these horrible news, the herald exits, while the elders wonder about the indifference Zeus has shown towards his own son.

After a few hours Heracles wakes up. He is told what he has done and, full of shame and desperation, is contemplating committing suicide. However, at this critical moment his friend Theseus arrives from Athens, to help him against the usurper Lycus. Amphitryon informs him about what has happened. Theseus sees Heracles among the corpses, hiding his face in shame. He tells him to uncover his face and find the courage to live on accepting the divine blows.

Heracles is sure that there is nowhere he can go where he will be accepted, being the murderer of his own children. Theseus, however, repeating that he must withstand his sufferings, invites him to Athens, where he will purify him from the murders. In addition to his hospitality, he promises him gifts of fields and treasures. Heracles decides to accept his fate and continue living, so that he is not remembered as a coward. He agrees to accept the invitation and, after assigning the burial duties to Amphitryon departs, as the chorus is bidding him farewell, calling him the best of their friends.

THE SUPPLIANTS
(AESCHYLUS)

The stage is a landscape outside of Argos. Near a hill with altars of gods stands the chorus, consisting of the Danaids, the daughters of Danaus, as suppliants. They have come here from Egypt, chased by their cousins, the sons of king Aegyptus, who want to marry them against their will. The suppliants are asking the Argives to offer them protection and release them from the yoke of the marriage with the sons of Aegyptus. They also call their ancestor Zeus for help, being the king of the gods, and also Artemis, the goddess of hunting, to ask for help from virgin to fellow virgin.

Danaus appears and, watching a crowd approaching, advises his daughters to gather next to the altars, holding branches of supplication and keeping in mind that they must be very careful, speak prudently and with the signs of supplication evident. The chorus runs towards the altars, while Pelasgus, the king of Argos, enters the stage. Initially, the chorus does not recognise him. He asks them who they are and where they come from, as their clothing betrays them as foreigners. The Danaids mention their Argive female ancestor Io, who had slept with Zeus. The jealous wife of Zeus, goddess Hera, turned Io into a cow. As Zeus continued his encounters with Io, Hera ordered Argos to guard her and sent Oestrus, the horsefly, to torment Io with his stinging in order to drive her away. Eventually, chased by Oestrus, Io ended up in Egypt.

Pelasgus at first doubts their Argive ancestry but is persuaded by all the details provided. When he asks them what exactly it is that they are requesting from him they inform him of their pursuers and implore him for protection. Pelasgus tells them that this is their conflict and not his and for this reason, he hesitates. He fears that if he helps them, as he likes to do with foreigners and suppliants, he would be brought in a confrontation with their pursuers. He thinks that the discontent that will be caused could even result in a war with Egypt. On the other hand, he also fears the wrath of Zeus, who is the protector of suppliants. As a king, he believes he has no right to cause such a misfortune to his subjects. But the Danaids insist, their persistence at times bordering on blackmailing. If he does not offer them protection, they threaten that they will hang themselves from the statues of the gods, a terrible miasma for the city. The king, as he has often said during their conversation, feels that the best solution would be to leave the decision to the hands of the people, so he decides to call a gathering. As he exits he adds that he will try to influence public opinion in their favour.

A short time later, Danaus returns bringing the decision of the Argive people: they will offer refuge and protection to the women, who will be able to live in Argos safe and free. The daughters of Danaus are full of good wishes for their protectors. However, Danaus warns that he can see enemy ships approaching. The Danaids once again are full of fear, lest the sons of Aegyptus come out of the ships and catch them.

Soon the sailors come out of the ships. They address their speech mainly through a herald but directly to the Danaids, requesting their surrender. They threaten that if they do not follow them obediently they will pull them from their hair and even decapitate them. As they continue with their threats the king appears and stresses that, although the herald is a foreigner, he did not request to be granted his rights from a local and by failing to do so he is showing disrespect towards the gods. The herald replies that they only want what rightfully belongs to them and that the only gods he respects are the gods of the Nile. The king expels the herald who threatens war.

As the Egyptian sailors depart, Pelasgus calms the daughters of Danaus by saying that Argos is a safe city guarded by walls and decrees that they should go to the various houses of the city that will offer them hospitality. The chorus wishes them a favourable outcome, stressing that the selection of the houses that they will stay at will be made by their father, their indisputable protector and counsellor. Pelasgus exits with his escort and Danaus comes in suggesting they should be grateful and honour the Argives. He also urges his daughters to be careful not to be disgraced, as they are at an age when they are particularly attractive to men. Aphrodite encourages men to gather the flower of the beautiful virgins, so his daughters must be careful not to give in to what they have so hard tried to avoid. The chorus assures him that he does not even need to mention the danger and that his daughters will never change their behaviour. Once again, they offer their best wishes to their protectors, the Argives, and they pray to goddess Artemis not to force them into a lawless marriage.

A chorus of female servants appears on stage glorifying Aphrodite as one of the goddesses with the most power. They foretell storms and wars, and wonder who helped the Egyptians in their voyage to come so fast after the Danaids. They advise moderation and say that perhaps it would have been for the best if the Danaids had accepted the marriage proposals of their cousins. The daughters stubbornly end the play by praying to Zeus to protect them from a loathsome marriage with any men, who they see as their adversaries.

THE SUPPLIANTS
(EURIPIDES)

The scene is set in Eleusis, in the temple of Demeter. In front of the temple's altar stands Aethra, the mother of Theseus, king of Athens. Joining her are the mothers of the seven dead leaders of the Argives who were killed during Polynices' expedition against his brother Eteocles, which took place following Eteocles' refusal to share the throne with him. Adrastus, the king of Argos and leader of the aforementioned expedition, is also there, standing in front of the altar next to the women and a few young men.

The mothers of the dead leaders, who comprise the chorus, wail holding branches of supplication because the victors of the war are not allowing them to take the bodies of their dead sons. Aethra's prayer to Demeter to help them is added to theirs. She has already sent a message to her son Theseus to come to assist the suppliants.

Theseus appears. His mother tells him who the women are, that the old man is Adrastus and the young men are the sons of the dead. Adrastus falls on his knees and begs him for help. Theseus tells him that the war was his mistake and that he ignored the foretellings of the seer Amphiaraus, which predicted their defeat. The head of the chorus intervenes and asks him to forgive Adrastus. Adrastus, however, making his annoyance at the Athenian king's criticism apparent, tells the women to stop. They do not, their leader reminding Theseus that they are relatives.

Aethra intervenes, kneeling in front of him and begging him with tears in her eyes. Theseus is persuaded by her words and agrees that it is right to help those who suffer injustice and an honour to respect customs which are valued all over the country, such as honouring the dead. He promises that he will ask the Thebaeans for the bodies, and if they refuse he will use force. He goes to the citizens' gathering to have his plan approved and returns armed and accompanied by soldiers. He gives orders to a herald to travel to Thebes to deliver his message. Before he has the chance to depart however, a foreign herald arrives and asks to see the king of the city. The Thebaeans are asking him to expel Adrastus and not to attempt to take the dead, threatening war. Theseus answers that Creon, the king of Thebes, is no more powerful than him and cannot force Athens to obey his orders; it is their duty to hand over the dead bodies. If they do not accept, he will use his army.

The herald departs. Theseus leaves too, to start preparations for the attack. Only Adrastus with the women remain on stage.

An Argive herald arrives from Thebes, announcing that Theseus and his cavalry have arrived in Thebes where they found the army waiting for them in front of the city walls.

Then a herald of Theseus came forward and announced that the Athenians had no intention to embark on a war and that they would not attack if the Thebaeans gave them the bodies of the dead, as they were rightfully requesting. Creon, however, initiated an attack but the Athenians emerged victorious. Even though Theseus could enter the castle he chose not to, stating that the purpose of his expedition was not to loot the city, but simply to take the dead and give them a proper burial.

The head of the chorus announces that the funeral procession is approaching. Soldiers appear, carrying the dead. Adrastus shares information about the killed leaders, praising each one of them separately. Theseus, Adrastus and the sons of the leaders follow the procession. When they reach the point where the bodies are about to be thrown in the fire, Evadne appears, the daughter of nobleman Iphis and wife of Capaneus, one of the seven dead leaders. She ascends on a rock behind the fire, ready to throw herself in. Iphis tries to change her mind but in vain and he becomes an eye witness of Evadne's suicide. The chorus wails at the death of the woman. Iphis departs in desperation, saying that he will lock himself up in his house, never to go out again.

Theseus, Adrastus and the sons return, the youngsters carrying an urn each. They are talking about revenge, which they wish to be able to take in the future. Goddess Athena appears, she advises Theseus to ask the Argives to promise under oath that they will never attack the city of Athens, before handing to the children the ashes of their fathers. She also speaks to the children, telling them that they will be the ones to take revenge when they grow up. She adds that their leader will be Aegialeus, Adrastus' son, and that his brave army will capture Thebes. They all declare their obedience to her orders.

HIPPOLYTUS
(EURIPIDES)

We are in the Peloponnese, outside the Troezen palace, in front of the altars and statues of Aphrodite and Artemis. Aphrodite, the goddess of love appears. She says that Hippolytus, son of king Theseus with the Amazon, is a worshipper of the hunting goddess Artemis and of the chastity she represents, and an adversary of Aphrodite. Aphrodite will punish him by tempting Phaedra, his father's new wife, to fall unlawfully in love with him. The queen is to keep her love secret, however Aphrodite's plan is for it to be eventually revealed so that Theseus kills his son.

Aphrodite exits the stage and Hippolytus appears together with his hunting companions. His companions comprise the first group of the chorus. They exalt Artemis and Hippolytus offers a wreath to the goddess, ignoring Aphrodite's statue. An old servant comes out of the palace; he advises Hippolytus that it is improper not to honour both goddesses equally, but his efforts are in vain.

As Hippolytus and his companions enter the palace, the second group of the chorus made up of Troezenian maidens comes out of the palace's doors. They say that Phaedra, the wife of Theseus, is ill from an unknown disease and has not been able to get out of bed for three days.

After a while, the old nurse of the queen leaves the palace along with Phaedra. The nurse asks her what is wrong and she answers that a divine curse has fallen upon her, a sickness of the mind. It is a sickness caused by her love for Hippolytus. She has tried to resist but it has developed into an illness that is torturing her and she no longer knows what to do. She fears her love will be revealed, which would be a disgrace both for her husband and also her children. She would rather kill herself. The chorus and the nurse understand her frustration, but find her reaction excessive. The old nurse advises her that perhaps she could find relief if she would tell Hippolytus what torments her, but Phaedra refuses. The nurse exits to bring her herbs to soothe her pain.

Hippolytus can be heard shouting from inside the palace. He is angry with the nurse for revealing to him Phaedra's secret love, after she put him under oath to keep what she told him a secret. Hippolytus and the nurse come out of the palace. Phaedra falls on her knees, begging him but he continues to shout, full of anger. He turns against all women, saying that it was a great mistake of Zeus to send them among men. Hippolytus exits saying that if he had not taken an oath, he would go to his father and tell him everything.

Phaedra turns against the nurse, who eventually leaves full of fear. Phaedra decides to commit suicide but states that her death will bring misfortune to somebody else, proving to them that they should not have bragged about her misery. She enters the palace and moments later screams can be heard from the nurse, who has just found the queen hanged.

Theseus comes in. When he is informed that the queen has committed suicide, he wails, wondering what led her to take her own life. He asks the chorus, but they claim that they are not aware. The answer to his perplexity is given by a letter in the hand of his dead wife. When Theseus reads it, his sorrow and wailing are overtaken by anger and wrath: his son dared to insult his nuptial chamber. He asks Poseidon, the god of the sea and his own father, to fulfil one of the three wishes he had granted him and kill his son before sunset. Before his death, Theseus also exiles Hippolytus from his country; this way he can be certain that at least one of the two evils will definitely happen.

Hippolytus comes in with his companions and asks what is going on. Theseus sneers at him: is he the pure man he pretends to be, enjoying the company of the gods? He tells him about the letter and announces his decision to exile him. Hippolytus insists that he has no idea about any of this and he swears that he has never approached a woman and that he is chaste. As Theseus is not persuaded, Hippolytus considers revealing the truth to him, but realises that he would not be believed and he would break his oaths to no avail. He eventually realises that there is nothing he can do and leaves the city.

Soon a herald arrives announcing that Hippolytus is close to his death: he had an accident with his chariot near

Corinth. Theseus thinks that the god answered his prayers. The herald continues saying that no one understood exactly what had happened; a noise was heard and from the angry sea a furious bull emerged, frightening the horses. The horses bolted, overturned the chariot which they kept towing, dragging Hippolytus and bashing him on the stone road. He was already nearly dead when help arrived. Theseus asks for his son to be brought to him.

A companion of Hippolytus carries him to the king. Goddess Artemis appears and they talk in front of Theseus, who at last understands his error. Artemis says that everything was planned by Aphrodite to punish Hippolytus for the lack of respect he showed towards her. The son speaks to his father softly, saying that he understands that he condemned him out of anger. Artemis promises Hippolytus that she will take revenge on his behalf by killing one of Aphrodite's loyal followers.

The tragedy ends with the death of Hippolytus, who passed away after forgiving his father, thus releasing him from the stigma of murder.

IPHIGENIA IN AULIS
(EURIPIDES)

Agamemnon, the king of Mycenae, is standing sleepless in front of his tent at the Achaean camp in Aulis. He says that according to an oracle, in order for the wind to blow so their ships can depart for the Trojan War, his daughter Iphigeneia has to be sacrificed. His brother Menelaus persuaded him to accept this, despite his serious objections. He also mentions that the reason for this military expedition was his brother's wife, Helen, who eloped with Paris, the prince of Troy. Agamemnon sent a fake message to his wife Clytemnestra, telling her that Iphigeneia should join him because he had decided to marry her with Achilles, the famous hero.

Next to the sleepless Agamemnon stands the old trusted slave of Clytemnestra. Agamemnon reveals to the old man that the marriage with Achilles is actually a lie and that he has decided to send him with a new message to his wife, telling her not to send Iphigeneia over as the marriage would allegedly take place at a later date. He also orders him to tell his daughter to return to her mother if they meet somewhere on his way to Mycenae.

Shortly after, Menelaus rushes in holding the letter with Agamemnon's message to his wife in his hands. He reads it and refuses to allow the old slave to leave. The two men argue and Agamemnon enters.

A heated dispute between the two brothers follows. Agamemnon accuses Menelaus of ambushing his emissary and opening a letter that was not addressed to him. Menelaus accuses Agamemnon of initially begging to be the expedition leader and willingly accepting the sacrifice of his daughter, and then changing his mind. This change of mind will make him the object of ridicule amongst the troops. Agamemnon replies that all this is happening so Menelaus can take back an unfaithful woman and he should not be the one who has to sacrifice his children. Menelaus accuses him of treason and prepares to depart but before he does, a herald comes in to announce the arrival of Clytemnestra, Iphigeneia and Agamemnon's young son, Orestes. Agamemnon is left alone and starts wailing, wondering how to confront his wife and what to tell his daughter. Menelaus, seeing his brother's distress, changes his mind. He asks Agamemnon to forgive him and not to sacrifice his daughter. Agamemnon says that either Calchas the seer or Odysseus will reveal to the army both the oracle and the fact that he took his promise back. The two brothers reconcile and Agamemnon finally takes the decision to sacrifice Iphigeneia.

Clytemnestra enters the stage with her children. Mother and daughter ask Agamemnon for details regarding the marriage and groom. When Agamemnon is left alone with his wife he asks her to return to Argos, telling her that a military camp is no place for a woman. When Clytemnestra refuses, Agamemnon departs to find Calchas so they can come up with a plan of how to sacrifice Iphigeneia.

Achilles appears, looking for Agamemnon. He speaks to Clytemnestra, who mentions her daughter's marriage to him and it becomes apparent that this is something Achilles is completely unaware of. Clytemnestra's old slave comes in and reveals to them the decision regarding Iphigenia's sacrifice. Clytemnestra panics and asks Achilles for help. He promises to help her, especially as unbeknown to him, his name was involved in such an ignominious plot. But he says that she should first beg her husband to change his mind, and exits the stage.

Agamemnon appears, asking Clytemnestra to tell their daughter to prepare for the bridal sacrifices to goddess Artemis. Clytemnestra bursts into tears and tells him that both her and Iphigeneia are aware of the horrible truth. She hurls accusations to him, starting from when he took her by force from her first husband, killing him and taking the child she had with him. She says that despite all of this she forgave him and from then on had always been a perfect wife. She ends by telling him that if he agrees with what she has said to him, he should not sacrifice their child. Iphigeneia also begs her father. Agamemnon faces a great dilemma. However eventually, he decides that if he does not go ahead with the sacrifice, the army, having run out of patience from being unable to sail for months will kill all of them in their rage, including his daughters at home in Argos. He decides that this sacrifice is not for Menelaus and Helen, but for the whole country which is asking it of him and unfortunately he cannot avoid it.

As Iphigeneia starts lamenting, Achilles comes in and announces that everybody in the army, even his own soldiers, are asking for Iphigeneia's sacrifice and threaten to stone Achilles for expressing his opposition. He is, nevertheless, determined to do his best. Listening to Achilles, Iphigeneia takes a great decision; she does not want to be the reason Achilles' life is in danger, and as the whole of Greece depends on her sacrifice she agrees to it. Achilles expresses his admiration for her and insists that he wants to save her and take her as his wife. Clytemnestra wails and Iphigeneia repeats that she is willing to be sacrificed and departs.

After a while, a herald comes in and announces that during the sacrifice Iphigeneia's body disappeared and was miraculously replaced by a beautiful doe. Calchas immediately declared to the army that it was certain that the goddess would now be in favour of the expedition. Clytemnestra is wondering what happened and who took her daughter before the sacrificial knife's touch. Agamemnon considers that things could not have turned out better and tells Clytemnestra that she should now take their other child and return home. He will go to Troy with his army and when the conflict is over he will return to Argos to live with them again.

The tragedy ends with the head of the chorus saluting Agamemnon as he departs for the Trojan War.

IPHIGENIA IN TAURIS
(EURIPIDES)

In front of a temple in the country of Tauris, Iphigeneia is describing how her father, Agamemnon, took her deceitfully from her mother Clytemnestra and sacrificed her to goddess Artemis, so that the weather would change and allow the departure of the Greek fleet for Troy. However, at the last minute Artemis took her from the altar and replaced her with a doe. She then brought her to Tauris, a barbaric country ruled by king Thoas. In this country any Greek found was immediately arrested and sacrificed to Artemis; Iphigeneia herself is a priestess in the temple of Artemis, responsible for preparing those who are about to be sacrificed. Iphigeneia is heard speaking about the dream she had the previous night: she was back in Argos, her home country, and while sleeping she was suddenly awaken by a powerful earthquake. She saw her whole house collapse, with only one column remaining intact; then, mourning, she started preparing the column to be sacrificed. She concludes that the column symbolises the male child of the family, Orestes. Since every person she prepares for sacrifice dies, Orestes must have, in real life, also died. She decides to offer libations in his memory and enters the temple to look for the women who will assist her.

Orestes appears, having just arrived in Tauris along with his friend Pylades. He prays to god Apollo and says that following the oracle he received, he killed his own mother and has since then been persecuted by the Furies. Once again following Apollo's directions, he has now come to Tauris in order to steal the statue of the goddess Artemis and bring it to the Athenians. Apollo has told him that this way his persecution by the Furies will cease. He sees the tall walls of the temple and is discouraged. Pylades insists that they must respect the oracle, and persuades his friend to hide in a cave and wait for the night to fall.

The chorus appears, a group of female slaves from Greece. A shepherd comes in and announces that they have caught two foreigners near the sea and they will bring them to the temple for sacrifice. As Iphigeneia is waiting for the foreigners she expresses her view that she does not believe that the goddess really requires all these human sacrifices, but rather the local people seem to be thirsty for blood and attribute their wishes to the goddess.

The two men are brought in tied up. When Iphigeneia learns that one of them comes from Argos, having not recognised Orestes, without revealing her name she asks for news from her family. When she learns that Orestes is alive, full of joy she proposes to the stranger to set him free if he agrees to deliver a letter to her family. Orestes proposes to have his friend deliver the letter instead, so that he is the one to be saved; he will be sacrificed in his place. Following some initial objections, Pylades accepts. Iphigeneia brings the letter, but she also reads it out loud to make him aware of its contents in case it gets lost. In the letter, she tells Orestes to come and rescue his sister Iphigeneia, who is not dead as everyone believes. Orestes, full of joy reveals his identity to Iphigeneia. She does not believe him and asks for evidence. When he gives her details about their family life she is persuaded and they talk about the good old days, full of emotion and tenderness towards one another. Orestes tells her about their mother's murder, which he committed in order to take revenge for the murder of their father. He also tells her about the Furies, the deities of the underworld who have been persecuting him following the murder and about Apollo, who sent him to stand trial in Athens in order to be acquitted and relieved from their persecution. In Athens he was indeed acquitted, but some of the Furies did not obey the decision of the court and continue to chase him. He has come to Tauris after Apollo's suggestion to steal the statue of Artemis so that he is relieved from their persecution.

Iphigeneia contrives a plan and asks the chorus not to reveal anything. She adds the promise that, when they return to Greece she will take care of them.

King Thoas comes in and Iphigeneia tells him that the statue of the goddess has been moved from its usual position so it stands as far as possible from the foreigners. They are too impure, as they have killed one of their mothers with their own bare hands. Therefore they must be cleansed, together with the statue, at a remote shore. She adds that for these reasons it would be improper for the local citizens to meet the foreigners. Thoas is persuaded and asks one of his followers to announce that no-one is allowed out in the streets while the foreigners and Iphigeneia pass through the city.

After a while, a herald enters. He reveals that the foreigners escaped together with Iphigeneia and the statue, boarding on a Greek ship. When Thoas learns that one of the foreigners was Orestes, he becomes furious and decides to pursue and arrest them at any cost.

However, goddess Athena appears and tells Thoas to stop the preparations for the pursuit. Everything has happened following an oracle by Apollo; even Poseidon, the god of the sea, supported the escape of the foreigners by calming the open sea. The goddess also speaks to Orestes, her divine voice being heard everywhere: he must go to Athens and build a temple where he is to place the statue. Iphigeneia will continue to be a priestess of goddess Artemis, this time in a temple located on the hills of Vravrona. Finally she orders Thoas to set the chorus free. Thoas obeys, as it is all the goddess' will .

I O N
(EURIPIDES)

In front of Apollo's temple in Delphi, god Hermes, the messenger of the gods, appears. He tells us that once upon a time in a cave near Athens, Apollo raped Creusa, the daughter of king Erechtheus of Athens. A child was born, which Creusa abandoned in that same cave to die. But Apollo ordered Hermes to take the baby and bring it to Delphi where he placed the newborn at the entrance of the temple. Pythia, the foreteller, found and nursed the baby. Now the baby has grown into a man, who is the treasurer of the temple.

In the meantime, Creusa married Xuthus, but did not have any children with him So, they have come here in Delphi to ask for advice from god Apollo as to what they can do to have a child.

A young man, Ion, comes out of the temple exalting Apollo. Having been brought up in the temple, he regards him as his father and is happy to serve him.

A chorus of Creusa's slaves comes. They are already in conversation with Ion when Creusa appears. She speaks of her infertility, while Ion tells her that he does not know who his parents are. Creusa says she is here to ask the oracle about a friend of hers, who had had an illegitimate child with Apollo; she had abandoned it and later on when she went to search for it, she could not find it. So her friend seeks to learn from the gods whether the child is alive or dead.

Xuthus goes to receive the oracle from the god. Meanwhile, Ion approaches Apollo and tells him it is not right to lure virgins into sleeping with him, and then when they give birth to illegitimate children to abandon them to cope with the consequences alone. How is it possible for the gods, who define the laws, to behave so unlawfully?

Xuthus comes out of the temple. He grasps Ion, and full of emotion announces to him that he is his son. He explains that the god had told him that the first person who he would meet would be his child. Ion asks about his mother, but Xuthus admits that as he was full of joy, he had forgotten to ask the god about the mother. Ion concludes that he must be the result of some relation when Xuthus was young and is emotional, because at least he has found his father. Xuthus proposes to take him to Athens. Ion, however, does not want to be known as an illegitimate child and for this reason prefers to stay in the temple. Xuthus then proposes to take Ion with him as an adopted son, and not as his biological child. At a later date, he will find the opportunity to reveal the truth to his wife. Ion accepts.

Creusa comes in with her old slave. The chorus informs her that her husband has found his son, thanks to the oracle. The old slave concludes that Xuthus must have had secret relations with a slave and had a son, whom he then gave to this temple to be raised. He was obviously only pretending when he claimed to have come to look for answers from the god. The old slave suggests that she should kill the illegitimate son.

Creusa, upon hearing of the alleged sin of her husband, decides to reveal to the old man that she had been raped by Apollo in a cave, where she had abandoned the fruit of their union. The old slave insists that she should kill Xuthus' son. She is persuaded and sends the slave to the celebration her husband is holding in the temple to drop poison to Ion's drink.

A while later, a slave appears, saying that they are looking for Creusa to stone her to death. King Xuthus was hosting a feast with Ion as his guest of honour. Then Creusa's old slave came in and filled everyone's cup with wine. However someone cursed and Ion, being pious, suggested that everyone should empty their cups and refill them. Then pigeons came and sipped from the wine that had fallen on the ground. The pigeon which sipped from Ion's wine died and all the guests then understood that the old man must have dropped poison in his cups, so they forced him to reveal who had ordered him to poison Ion. Then the rulers of Delphi decided to kill both Creusa as well as the chorus, collectively responsible for the attempted murder.

The chorus suggests to a terrified Creusa to go to the altar as a suppliant. Ion tries to arrest her with the help of soldiers. Pythia, the foreteller of Apollo, appears and mediates in order to save the woman, but Ion is not persuaded. Pythia then shows to him a small basket, telling him that she had found him in it when he was a baby. It was now time he searched for his mother. Then Creusa, full of surprise, recognises the basket. She attempts to leave the altar to embrace her son. He is hesitant but Creusa describes in detail the contents of the basket.She also reveals to him that his true father is god Apollo, who is happy to hand him to Xuthus to live in wealth, having a father and a respected family name. Ion does not believe he is Apollo's child.

Goddess Athena appears and tells Ion that she has come on behalf of Apollo and that everything Creusa has told him is true. She orders Creusa to take her child to Athens, where Ion will become king. His descendants will populate a large country which will take his name and be called Ionia. She also advises Creusa not to reveal the truth to Xuthus, letting him believe what Apollo's oracle had told him and allowing him to be happy. Before leaving, Athena stresses the fact that gods may sometimes take long, but they never forget to settle their obligations.

The tragedy ends with the chorus stating that good people always find justice in the end, if they respect the gods.

MEDEA
(EURIPIDES)

We are in Corinth, in front of the house where Medea lives with her children. A nurse comes out and declares that if the expedition of the Argonauts had not taken place, her lady would not have met Jason and fallen in love with him. She would not have married him, nor would they have been forced to take refuge in Corinth where king Creon rules. After they arrived here the king offered them his hospitality and Medea's husband fell in love with the king's daughter, Glauce. Now the nurse fears that Medea may decide to take revenge, as she has a violent nature.

The kids' pedagogue comes bringing to the nurse the news that Creon is planning on expelling Medea and her children. Medea, who is inside the house, unaware of the conversation, wails so loudly that can be heard from the outside. She shouts that she even killed her own brother as a favour to Jason and curses everyone who has ever wronged her, even her own children. A chorus of Corinthian women appears and the nurse persuades Medea to come out of the house. Medea tells the chorus that she has found herself all alone in a distant land and is facing the contempt and abandonment of the man she had followed. She asks them as a favour not to betray her if she finds a way to punish the fornicator.

Creon appears, and says that Medea must depart immediately so that she does not have time to harm him, his daughter or Jason. Medea calmly tries to change his mind to allow her to stay in town, but in vain. She finally asks him to give her one more day to make the necessary preparations for her children. The king agrees.

However, Medea is a witch and as she reveals, just one day is more than enough to take her revenge. Her only worry is that after her revenge no country will give her refuge. But no enemy of hers will remain unpunished and she takes a vow in the name of Hecate, the goddess witch whom she worships more than any other deity.

Jason enters the stage and quickly gets into an argument with Medea. She reminds him of all the assistance she has given him and how she abandoned her father and country for him. He replies that it was Aphrodite, the goddess of love, who helped him and tells her that she should be happy that she, a barbarian, is now residing in Greece and has become famous for her wisdom. He also tells her that the reason he married the daughter of a king was to give Medea and their children the opportunity to live comfortably. He even offers her money for when she leaves for exile and Medea becomes furious. Their conversation ends with her jeering at Jason.

Aegeus, the king of Athens, appears. Medea promises him that she, as a witch, will solve the problem of his childlessness. In return she asks from him to swear that he will accept her in his land and he will never expel her, even if an enemy requests him to. Aegeus makes a promise to her and their meeting ends.

Medea reveals her plan to the chorus, which tries to change her mind: she will ask Jason to keep their children and let her leave Corinth alone. She will offer Jason's new wife a fine-wrought robe and a golden wreath as a gift, in order to persuade her to keep the children. These gifts will be covered in poison strong enough so that when she wears them she will be killed, together with anyone who tries to help her. After that, she will also kill her children so that Jason remains childless.

Jason enters and Medea, speaking charmingly, persuades him to ask his new wife to keep the children and sends her the lethal presents. When the pedagogue informs Medea that the king's daughter has accepted, she begins to wail for her children. She is still hesitant, but as she confesses, anger overides all other thoughts in her mind: she is going to kill them.

The news of Glauce's death come soon. Her father, king Creon, is also dead, poisoned as he was trying to help her. Medea then enters the palace to kill her children. The chorus, horrified by what is about to happen, attempts to stop the heinous crime and calls the Sun and the Earth to mediate in changing Medea's mind. But nothing can change her plan and shortly after the cries of her children are heard from the palace.

Jason enters the stage. He has been informed about the fate of Glauce and her father and has come to protect his children from his wife's relatives' potential revenge. The head of the chorus informs him about the new crimes and he furiously rushes into the palace to kill the murderess. But as he tries to open the gate, Medea can be seen up high, on a chariot led by winged dragons with their dead children with her. She is too high for Jason to reach and a heated argument follows with each of them placing responsibility for the murders on the other. He asks her for the children's bodies so that he can bury them but she refuses. She will bury them with her own hands and from then on she will order an annual memorial ceremony that will remind everyone of Jason's immoral behaviour. She announces that she will leave for the country of Aegeus where she will be offered hospitality as it has been promised to her. Finishing her speech, Medea prophesies Jason's death. As a final entreaty Jason asks her to let him touch the bodies of his children, but Medea refuses.

OEDIPUS AT COLONUS
(SOPHOCLES)

Driven away from Thebes, Oedipus arrives together with his daughter Antigone to a place planted with sacred olives, laurels and vineyards. The area is unknown to them, but judging from the plants they assume that it is a holy place. A stranger appears and tells them they should leave because the place belongs to the Eumenidae, the terrible daughters of Darkness and Earth. They also learn that they are in Colonus, at the edge of the city of Athens, where Theseus is king. Oedipus is relieved to have arrived to the place where, according to an oracle by Apollo, his life will end along with his torments and asks the stranger to call the king.

A chorus of old Athenians enters the stage. They ask Oedipus to leave the sacred grove and he obeys. When they learn of his identity, they ask him to leave the country, but he replies that he is not to blame as he was ignorant of his actions. Besides, as a suppliant he has the right to be protected. The elders allow them to stay temporarily but the final decision lays with the king.

Ismene appears bringing bad news from Thebes: Oedipus' youngest song, Eteocles has usurped the throne from the eldest son, Polynices, and exiled him. Polynices went to Argos, where he summoned allies and he is now about to launch an expedition against Eteocles. According to an oracle, the Thebaens will manage to protect their city from the enemies only if Oedipus is present at the city borders, dead or alive. So Creon, their uncle, is on his way to bring Oedipus back to Thebes.

Oedipus curses his children for not helping prevent his exile and decides not to help either of them. Ismene leaves to prepare the offerings the chorus advises Oedipus to place.

Theseus arrives and Oedipus begs him to offer them hospitality, promising him that he will repay his services. However, he will not do it until immediately before his death and for this reason asks Theseus to be next to him at the moment of his death, when he will reveal what the gift he is promising to him is.

Creon appears intending to persuade Oedipus to return to Thebes, because, as he says, it is a shame for him to be wandering like a tramp. Oedipus accuses him of lying and tells him that he knows the real reason from an oracle. Creon threatens him: he has already arrested Ismene and he is going to take Antigone too. The cries of the elders bring Theseus back. He is informed about what is going on and makes it clear to Creon that he will not let him carry out his threats. An argument between Oedipus and Creon follows; while Creon knows that what he is blaming Oedipus for was done unknowingly, he accuses him for incestuous marriage and patricide. Theseus intervenes and asks Creon to reveal where

Ismene and Antigone are. Creon yields and is immediately expelled from Athens. Theseus tells Oedipus about a fellow Thebaean who wishes to speak to him. It is revealed that this is none other than his son Polynices and their meeting follows.

Polynices asks Oedipus to assist him with his military expedition against his brother as an oracle has said that the person who has Oedipus on their side will win. He reveals that he is ready to attack with the help of the Argive army, as he has married the daughter of the king of Argos. Oedipus, however, is angry both with Polynices for exiling him and also with Eteocles for not offering to help him. He refuses to participate in their war and curses both his children to kill each other. Polynices departs from Athens.

A thunder is heard and Oedipus, knowing from the oracle that his death is approaching, asks for Theseus. He states that he will lead Theseus to the place of his death and if Theseus keeps the place a secret he will forever have his help against enemy invasions. Great secrets will also be revealed to him which he will then be able to pass on to his successor.

A herald describes how Oedipus walked up to a certain point together with his daughters. He then asked Theseus to accompany him alone, asking his children to stay at a distance. After a while, Oedipus disappeared and Theseus was seen standing as if he had witnessed something unbearably horrible.

The tragedy ends with the two daughters asking to learn

where their father has been buried. Theseus refuses to disclose that information and the daughters ask for his permission to travel to Thebes so they can at least try to prevent their brothers' foretold death.

OEDIPUS REX
(EURIPIDES)

The population of Thebes is suppliant in front of the altars as a terrible pestilence has broken out, killing animals and destroying the crops. The king of Thebes, Oedipus, is talking to a priest who is delivering a plea on behalf of his subjects to help them end their misery. People believe that he is the only person capable of doing this, as he has done so in the past: he was the one who relieved them from the tax they had to pay to the Sphinx, a monster with the head and breasts of a woman, the wings of a bird and the legs and tail of a lion.

Oedipus replies that he has already sent Creon, his brother-in-law, to Delphi to receive an oracle regarding the way they should act. Creon appears and announces that god Apollo said that the country must be cleansed from the impurity of the murder of its former king, Laius and that the murderer must be persecuted.

Oedipus immediately offers a reward to anyone who gives relevant information and prohibits contact with the murderer, whose punishment will be exile. He sees it as his personal duty to discover who killed the previous husband of his wife Jocasta and promises that he will do everything in his power to find him.

The chorus proposes that Teiresias the seer should be called to reveal the murderer and Oedipus responds that he has already done so. Teiresias initially refuses to speak, saying that he would be revealing unpleasant secrets concerning the king himself. But pressurised by Oedipus, he reveals that the murderer is Oedipus, who had also committed incest.

Oedipus throws the seer out of the palace, while the men of the chorus doubt what they have heard. Oedipus believes that the words Teiresias spoke were put in his mouth by Jocasta's brother, Creon, who although an old and faithful friend of his, now has his eyes on the throne.

Creon arrives immediately to defend himself, but in spite of his reassurance Oedipus considers him a traitor and declares that he intends to kill him. Creon defends his innocence and swears to the gods that he knows nothing about what Oedipus is accusing him of. The chorus advises Oedipus to find proof that his accusations against Creon are valid, and that it is right to respect somebody's oaths to the gods.

Jocasta comes in and intervenes to save her brother from the accusations of Oedipus. In order to calm the king she tells him he does not need to fear the oracles too much, since they are often incorrect. As an example she mentions the oracle given to Laius, that he would be killed by his own child. In order to protect himself from the son that was born after this oracle, Laius drilled holes on his ankles, tied them together and threw the child on a mountain.

Oedipus starts suspecting that Teiresias may have been right and fears that he could be Laius' murderer. He reveals that while in Corinth once, he had heard that he was not the real child of Merope and king Polybus. So he went to Delphi to ask the oracle. The response did not reveal his true parents, but it did reveal that he was to marry his mother and kill his father. He did not return to Corinth in case the oracle came true. On his way he came across a carriage and a disagreement with its passengers led him to kill their leader. Feeling uneasy, Oedipus asks about the murder of Laius. He orders to find and bring before him a slave who he learns is the only survivor of the accident.

A herald appears and announces that Polybus, the king of Corinth, is dead. Oedipus feels sorrow but also relief as the fear that he might be the one who murders him was now over. He still fears that he might end up marrying Merope, so to avoid this he states that he has no intention of returning to Corinth. The herald tells him that he is right to fear such a thing, because Merope is not his true mother. He reveals that he had saved him when he was a baby: he had been given to him by a shepherd who found him on mount Cithaeron with his ankles tied together. In turn, he offered the baby for adoption to the childless pair of Polybus and Merope. When the slave who had witnessed the murder of Laius appears it is revealed that the biological parents of Oedipus were Jocasta and Laius, and that the murderer of Laius was indeed Oedipus. Jocasta enters the palace and a few minutes later a servant announces that she has strangled herself. He adds that when Oedipus saw her dead he approached her and thrust the golden brooches that secured her dress into his eyes to blind himself so he would be unable to witness his misfortunes and crimes. A blind Oedipus appears and asks the elders to kill or exile him.

Creon, whom Oedipus now acknowledges as the king, arrives and Oedipus asks him to exile him from the country. Creon replies that he will do so only after consulting a god.

The chorus addresses the people, reminding them that one's situation can be completely different in the beginning and at the end of one's life, and as an example point to the man standing in front of them.

ORESTES
(EURIPIDES)

In the palace of Atreides in Argos, next to the bed of Orestes, who is sleeping, stands his sister Electra. Apollo, she says, persuaded Orestes to kill his mother Clytemnestra as a punishment for his father's murder. Electra assisted him in this horrible crime together with his friend Pylades. Now Orestes is ill, while the people of Argos are persecuting them as matricides. The day of the decision on how they will be executed has arrived. Their only hope is that their uncle Menelaus, the king of Sparta, will help them. Menelaus will be coming to Argos following the arrival of his wife Helen, Clytemnestra's sister. She had arrived secretly to avoid being stoned by the Argives in revenge for all their children who had been lost in the Trojan War for which they considered Helen responsible. Their daughter Hermione is also there, having been a guest in Clytemnestra's palace for years.

Helen exits the palace and accuses god Apollo of the death of her sister. She asks about Orestes and wants Electra to go to her sister's tomb to pour libations, as she is afraid of revealing herself to the Argives. But Electra is also afraid to visit her mother's tomb, so eventually Hermione goes.

A chorus of Argive maidens appears, and asking Electra about the health of Orestes, they wake him. As the Furies start persecuting him again, Orestes admits that he slaughtered his mother but he blames Apollo, because it was Apollo's words that made him do it.

Menelaus appears on stage and says that he has been informed of his brother's murder by Clytemnestra and of Clytemnestra's murder by Orestes. Orestes repeats that he was obeying the will of god Apollo and asks Menelaus for his help, as the Argives are about to condemn them to death.

Tyndareus, Orestes' grandfather and former king of Sparta also arrives and accuses Orestes of murdering his daughter. Orestes insists that he committed the murder as revenge for the murder of his father. Tyndareus believes that no excuse in the world can justify his act and asks Menelaus to abstain from any attempt to save Orestes, threatening that otherwise he will not allow him to return to Sparta. Orestes continues trying but his words only anger his grandfather who decides to encourage the Argives to stone them to death. Orestes requests the help of Menelaus, as he has a duty both towards his father but also to them, as the Trojan War, the cause of all evils, took place because of his own wife, Helen. Menelaus seems to be persuaded by his words, but he has no army with him so he is unable to confront the Argives. He says that he will try to convince Tyndareus to assume a better stance towards Orestes. He leaves and Orestes, who was expecting more substantial help, accuses him of only knowing how to fight for a woman and not being capable of defending a friend.

Orestes' friend Pylades arrives saying that his father expelled him for participating in the heinous murder. He also announces the decision regarding their fate: Orestes and Electra are to be stoned to death. Orestes then goes to speak to the people's assembly himself, joined by Pylades, but the only thing they manage to achieve is to be granted permission to commit suicide instead of being stoned. Electra asks Orestes to kill her and to share the same tomb with her. He refuses, the murder of his mother is enough. Pylades declares that he wishes to die together with his friend but proposes that they first should punish Menelaus for his indifference in helping them. A suitable way to do so would be to murder Helen, as she should also pay a price for all she had caused Greece. Orestes agrees and Electra adds that they should take his daughter, Hermione, as a hostage so they could blackmail him in an attempt to save themselves. The two men enter the palace from where Helen's cries can soon be heard.

Electra has stayed out of the palace. On her way back from her visit to Clytemnestra's tomb Hermione comes across Electra. The two converse and Hermione promises to do whatever she can to help them save themselves. She then enters the palace to meet her mother.

A Phrygian slave of Helen comes out of the palace horrified and announces that Orestes was holding Helen by the hair and was ready to cut her throat, when she disappeared. He also says that Orestes and Electra, assisted by Pylades, took Hermione hostage so they could save themselves. Orestes pulls the Phrygian back into the palace to prevent him from notifying Menelaus.

However, Menelaus comes in, having already been informed about everything. He talks to Orestes who has climbed on the palace's roof, threatening to kill his daughter and burn the palace. The only way out for Menelaus, they tell him, is to go to the Argives and persuade them not to kill them. Then Apollo appears declaring that he was the one taking Helen from the hands of Orestes, after an order by Zeus, and has immortalised her. He adds that Orestes will travel to Athens where he will be judged and set free. He will then return to Argos where he will marry Hermione and rule the city and Pylades will marry Electra.

THE PERSIANS
(AESCHYLUS)

A chorus of Persian elders is standing in front of Xerxes' palace in Sousa. From what they say we learn that when Xerxes left for his military expedition he trusted them to guard his palaces for as long as he was absent. They add that they do not have any news about how the expedition is going and they worry for the large Persian army, which comprises "the flowers of Asia", as they call the men.

Queen Atossa appears on stage, she is Xerxes' mother and Darius' widow. Addressing the chorus she says that she has left her riches and palace behind and she is there to ask for their advice. She had a dream that both puzzled and worried her. She dreamt of two women, one wearing Persian clothing and the other Dorian. It seemed to her that the one had inherited Greece and the other their land. The two women were arguing and Xerxes was trying to subordinate them. Finally, he tied them on his chariot, but while the one was obedient, the other one broke the yoke in two pieces. Then Darius appeared trying to help his son. When he saw him, Xerxes tore his clothes in sorrow.

After this dream, the queen went to Apollo's altar where

she offered sacrifices to atone herself. While she was there, an eagle flew over the altar and was attacked by a falcon who was plucking the feathers off its head.

The elders advise Atossa to pray to the gods to exorcise the bad dream and to pour libations on Darius' grave, asking him to guard his son against all evils.

A Persian herald comes bringing the news that the Persian fleet was destroyed in Salamis; the shores of the island were full of corpses. They were defeated by a much smaller Athenian fleet, so he believes that the Athenian's victory was due to divine intervention. The elders and the herald wail. However, the herald adds that fortunately, while many famous Persian generals were killed, Xerxes himself is alive and well. The ordeal began with a false piece of information given by an alleged informant to Xerxes, that the Greek ships would secretly leave Salamis at night. He fell in a trap by believing him and ordered his fleet to gather there to prohibit the escape of the enemy fleet. But in the morning, having chosen the location for the naval battle, the Greeks attacked and the larger Persian ships were trapped in a narrow passage where they were so crowded they could not manoeuvre to defend themselves or even escape. Xerxes was watching from an elevated point, from which he could observe the details of the battle. When he saw the noble Persians on a nearby island being exterminated, he tore his clothes off, and ordering his land forces to retreat, he fled.

The queen starts lamenting: her son went to take revenge for his father's defeat at Marathon and instead he was punished in a horrible way. The herald finishes his narration by saying that the Persians who escaped death were on their way back, and having walked through many places, exhausted by hunger and thirst, had arrived at the river Strymon during the night. The gods had brought a heavy winter, freezing the river. The army started to walk on it, but when the sun came out the ice melted and many men fell in the water and drowned. Very few eventually reached Thrace, from where they finally returned to their country.

The elders criticise Xerxes for his inexperience and belligerent disposition which led the country to such a loss, while in contrast they speak about Darius with respect. Darius was always serious and had never acted in a way that harmed his people. The queen proposes to ask the spirit of Darius for help with the use of libations and sacrifices and the chorus obeys.

The ghost of Darius appears, shocking the elders. The ghost asks why people are wailing on his tomb. The queen informs him that the whole military power of the Persians, both the army and the navy has been destroyed by the Athenians. She mentions that they built a bridge over Hellespont for the army to pass, an act considered hostile by Darius (hubris) and against the gods, especially Poseidon, and she asks Darius what they should do now. She tries to excuse her son saying that he was influenced by friends who were comparing him to Darius and saying that, while his father amassed a lot of riches from his wars, he was just sitting at home doing nothing.

Darius advises never to attack the Greeks again, because they will never manage to defeat them. The Greek effort was assisted by the fact that many of the Persians died from hunger. But even the few Persians who have stayed back there will be defeated in Plataea. The ghost of the king accuses the Persian soldiers of sacrilege because they had destroyed Greek temples during their attacks. He also advises to admonish Xerxes when he returns so that he stops insulting the gods. The ghost of Darius disappears and Atossa enters the palace.

Xerxes appears, wailing for his personal misfortune, but also for the disaster that befell on the whole Persian world, feeling shame for the destruction of his fleet.

PROMETHEUS BOUND
(AESCHYLUS)

In Scythia, two of Zeus' servants, Strength and Violence, oversee Hephaestus who is binding Themis' son, Prometheus, tightly with chains for stealing the fire from the gods and giving it to the humans. Hephaestus is not comfortable tormenting a fellow god, but decides to do so. The chorus arrives on a flying chariot, comprised of the Oceanids, the daughters of Oceanus, who are lamenting Prometheus' misfortune. The only god who could be so cruel as to put him in such a torture could have been Zeus. Prometheus tells them that he hates the king of the gods, revealing that he will take his revenge when Zeus asks him who will be the new ruler to usurp his kingdom and he will not reveal the secret at any cost. Prometheus reminds them of how unfair Zeus is being to him, as it was based on his advice as well as that of his mother Themis that Zeus had defeated the old king of the gods, Zeus own father, Cronus.

The chorus asks Prometheus what he has done and why he is being punished in such a horrible way. He answers that he helped the mortals: he gave them fire, he relieved them from the fear of death and gave them hope. When the chorus asks for more details, Prometheus promises to tell them the whole story if they in turn assist him in his ordeal. The Oceanids agree, promising to offer him their help.

Oceanus appears on a winged creature. He too is a god and a relative of Prometheus. He advises moderation, saying that the new monarch is ruthless and irresponsible; Oceanus is willing to intercede so that Zeus sets him free. Prometheus, with some contempt, tries to avoid this, warning of the danger that Oceanus may also fall into disfavour, hurt by his good intentions. As he sees that his attempts have failed, Oceanus departs.

In the conversation between Prometheus and the chorus that follows, it is explained how Prometheus fell into the disfavour of the gods when he taught humans the arts of civilisation. The chorus tries to offer him some hope, but Prometheus replies that he knows that the time of his freedom has not come yet. Io appears on stage, transformed into a cow and pursued by a horsefly. Another of Zeus' victims, she is tormented by his wife Hera's jealousy. Io tells how Zeus was pursuing her with sexual dreams during the nights and finally used an oracle to make her father throw her out of the house, threatening that if he did not he would throw a thunderbolt to burn the family house down. Then she assumed her present form and has been wandering endlessly, stung by a divine horsefly sent by Hera. She asks Prometheus to tell her what her future holds. He prophesies that she will be wandering for a long time and describes her travels. He stresses the cruelty of Zeus, who in an attempt to enjoy her love has subjected her to a terrible torture for the rest of her life.

Seeking revenge, Io asks Prometheus to tell her more about the probable usurpers of Zeus' authority. He replies that things will change when a child of Zeus is born who, being wiser than him, will overthrow him. He adds that he will be unbound thirteen generations later by a descendant of hers. She will find rest in the Nile's country. There, from a mere touch by Zeus' hand, Epaphus will be born. Five generations later a descendant of Epaphus will have fifty daughters, who will return to Argos, leaving Egypt to escape their cousins' persistence to marry them. Out of the fifty, only one will not murder her husband and will give a new royal family to Argos. It is from this family that the saviour of Prometheus will be descended.

The chorus expresses their sympathy towards Io and wish never to suffer such a torment themselves. They pray to marry suitable men and not some god. They especially pray to avoid ever being forced to sleep with Zeus.

Hermes comes as a herald of Zeus, carrying an order to Prometheus to reveal which of the marriages will result in the loss of Zeus' throne. Prometheus says he does not fear the new gods; he has already witnessed the demise of two kings of the gods and he will now witness the third. He will reveal nothing unless he is set free. The reply of Hermes to the unyielding stance of Prometheus is a threat for new torments: Zeus will strike the rocks on which Prometheus is chained and he will be buried under their debris. When, after many years he sees the sun again, Zeus' eagle will visit him every day to eat his liver.

A scared chorus advises Prometheus to obey, but in vain. The tragedy ends with Prometheus announcing that the thunders of Zeus have started; it seems that Zeus' threats have started to materialise.

R H E S U S
(EURIPIDES)

Darkness prevails in the Trojan camp, Hector is sleeping in his tent. Guards come, forming the chorus, which is divided into two halves. Hector is woken up by their voices and is informed about suspicious movements in the Achaean camp. The guards fear that the Achaeans are preparing an attack, whist Hector is certain that they are planning on leaving in the middle of the night and his view is that he must pursue them. Aeneas appears fearing a probable trap and that the Achaeans are ready to fight. He advises prudence and the dispatch of a spy in order to discover the truth. Dolon offers himself as the spy; as a reward he wants the horses of Achilles.

A shepherd approaches announcing the arrival of a foreign general with a huge army. This general is Rhesus, the king of Thrace. Hector declares his annoyance by the delay of his arrival; he does not need friends who come when they see him winning. But the chorus advises him to accept the Thracian's participation, because his victory in this war is not certain yet.

Rhesus appears on stage and Hector reprimands him for

not coming earlier to help in the war effort, while without Hector's help he would have never been the king of Thrace. Rhesus replies that he was absent in another war and he came as soon as that finished. He may have arrived late, but he is certain that in a day he can accomplish more than the Trojans have accomplished in ten years. He asks Hector to tell him which one of the enemies is considered the most powerful so that he can kill him. Hector answers that, since Achilles is angry with the Achaeans and abstains from battle, he would have to choose Odysseus. Rhesus claims that he will bring Odysseus on a spit which he will place in front of the gates of Troy for the vultures to eat. Before they separate, Hector tells Rhesus that the secret password of his army is "Phoebus".

Odysseus appears together with Diomedes. In their conversation they reveal that they arrested Dolon and forced him to reveal the Trojan's password before killing him. They have come to the Trojan camp to kill Hector, but cannot find him. They are ready to leave when goddess Athena, a supporter of the Greeks, suddenly appears in front of them. She reveals to them that Rhesus has come to help Hector and if he is not destroyed, the Greeks will lose the war. The two men decide to kill him and take his splendid chariot and horses. They exit the stage.

Paris appears in front of Hector's tent, and thinking his brother is inside, announces to him that he was informed that an Achaean spy has penetrated their army. Goddess Athena transformed into Aphrodite, an ally of the Trojans, reassures him that there is no reason to worry. Paris calms down and leaves. When Athena is alone, she speaks to Odysseus. He and Diomedes have killed Rhesus and have taken his horses, but the enemies have discovered this and are already searching for them. They must leave immediately. The goddess disappears.

Some guards are persecuting Odysseus and Diomedes. Odysseus assures them he is a friend and to prove it gives them the password "Phoebus". He adds that he saw foreigners running through the night and sent them to the opposite direction, so that they could escape.

Rhesus' charioteer appears; he is wounded and walks with difficulty. He talks to the head of the chorus and brings bad news of the murder of his master and the theft of his horses.

At this point Hector enters running, full of anxiety. He has been informed about the intruders and threatens the guards with heavy punishment, even beheading, for their negligence. The charioteer, however, accuses Hector. To them, he is the main suspect, as he is the only person they know here. The Thracians came here to offer him their help and he killed them in order to seize their horses along with the famed chariot of their king. Hector defends himself by saying that nobody has ever accused him of such things. He offers the charioteer his hospitality and he sends a message to his father, the king Priam, regarding the burial of the dead.

High in the sky a goddess appears: she is the muse Terpsichore, Rhesus' mother. She is holding her dead son in her arms. She wails and curses Odysseus, as she knows that he is the one responsible for his death. The chorus joins in her wailing, as is the custom for a dead stranger. The muse also curses Diomedes and says that, while these two were the killers, she knows that the true instigator was Athena. The chorus realises that Hector was accused unjustly. The hero addresses Terpsichore, telling her that he will bury Rhesus with royal honours. The muse responds that earth will not take her son. She will ask Persephone to leave his soul there, in the caves. She prophesies the death of Achilles and then disappears. Hector remains on stage and orders that everyone should prepare for battle immediately. He is sure that this is the day he will defeat the enemy and burn their ships.

The tragedy ends with the head of the chorus urging the soldiers to execute Hector's command as soon as possible and prepare for battle, in which he hopes the gods will help them and at last lead them to victory.

THE TRACHINIAE
(SOPHOCLES)

The scene is set outside the house where Deianira, the wife of Heracles, is offered hospitality in Trachis, in central Greece. Deianira is complaining to her nurse about her unfortunate life. When she was still living in her parental home, she was afraid they would marry her to Achelous, the river god who was changing form and was sometimes a man with a face of an ox and sometimes a dragon-like snake. However, Heracles came, and defeating Achelous, won her as his wife. Deianira then thought that her misfortunes were over, but even as Heracles' wife she was living a life full of anxiety. Most of the time her husband was away from her carrying out his labours, just as he was now.

The nurse proposes that she should tell Hyllus, her oldest son, to find news of his father from whom they have not had any word for several months. When Deianira contacts Hyllus, he informs her that he already knows that his father was a slave to a woman for a whole year and that at the time he was campaigning against the city of Eurytus, in Euboea. Deianira asks him to go to his father for help and when he departs she shares her worries with the chorus. Before leaving, Heracles had given her a specific order: if he had not returned within fifteen months they should consider him dead.

A herald appears, bringing good news. He has just heard from Lichas, the public crier, that Heracles is alive and will appear soon. Lichas comes, confirms what the herald said and adds that the hero's delay was due to his subordination to queen Omphale, an order by Zeus, and his subsequent desire for vengeance. The reason for his slavery was Eurytus, who while having him as a guest, had terribly offended him and had thrown him out of his palace. Then Heracles murdered his son Iphitus, thus invoking the wrath of Zeus. As soon as Heracles was free again, he summoned up an army and in turn returned to enslave Eurytus and his family. He conquered his city and enslaved its women, whom he had had now brought here with him. Deianira feels sorrow looking at these women, especially a noble-looking young maiden; she asks Lichas who she is but receives no answer.

The herald reveals Lichas' lies to Deianira. The girl she had asked about was Iole, the daughter of Eurytus, and she was the true reason for the wrath of Heracles, as he had asked Eurytus to give her to him to keep as a secret concubine and the king had refused. So Heracles campaigned against him, conquered his city, killed him and took Iole with him, together with other women. Lichas returns, and being pressed by Deianira confesses the truth, stressing that the previous lies were his own initiative, and he exits the stage. Deianira explains to the chorus that the behaviour of Heracles may be due to an illness and that she does not hate him. She does fear however that she will probably not be able to compete with the young and beautiful Iole. She remembers that she is in possession of a magic philtre given to her by Centaur Nessus. It was the first time she was following Heracles on a journey when they were about to pass a river. Nessus was carrying people to the other bank on his back. He was carrying Deianira when, in the middle of the river, he started fondling her body. Heracles who was following them aimed at Nessus and hit him with one of his arrows, which were poisoned by the black bane from the Lernaean Hydra's gall. Before dying, Nessus told her to collect blood from his wound and keep it in a place away from sunlight. He told her that this is a love potion so strong that she would never lose Heracles to another woman.

Deianira then asks Lichas to offer Heracles a thin mantle she had smeared over with the philtre as a gift. After Lichas' departure, Deianira notices that the wool with which she had smeared the mantle dissolved when thrown in the sunlight, and the only thing that remained was ashes. She starts worrying that instead of good, she might cause him harm and fears that Nessus may have given her a poison to kill Heracles. If such a horrible thing was to happen, she would follow her husband to death.

Hyllus appears full of wrath, bringing the bad news: the mantle proved to be a "deadly veil". When his father put it next to his flesh and went to make a sacrifice, the mantle stuck on him and began hurting him. When Lichas tried to assure him that he was innocent and that Deianira had sent the mantle for him, he killed him by throwing him on a rock. Then he called Hyllus and asked him to take him far away from people. He brought his father back, and thinking that his mother was responsible, curses her to be punished by the Furies. Deianira leaves and the nurse later finds her dead inside the house.

When Hyllus finds out the truth about his mother's mistake, he repents for his curses. Heracles appears on the stage nearly dead, in terrible plain. He wants to punish Deianira, but finds out about her innocence and her subsequent death. He remembers an old oracle, that said he would be killed by a dead person, and being convinced his time has come, orders Hyllus to take an oath he will do whatever he asks him to. He then asks him to collect branches and burn him with them, to relieve him from the pain. Hyllus agrees to do everything except ignite the fire, as he does not want to be his father's killer. Heracles also asks him to take Iole as his wife. Hyllus refuses but, as Heracles threatens him with the gods' curse, he finally agrees, speaking angrily against the indifference of the gods.

THE TROJAN WOMEN
(EURIPIDES)

After the end of the Trojan War, Poseidon, the god of the sea, appears on the seashore of Troy, sorrowful that Troy has been destroyed. Athena, the goddess of wisdom, joins him. She complains that the Achaeans, who were enjoying her support, desecrated her temple when Ajax seized the priestess Cassandra who had come there as a suppliant, and not even one Achaean tried to stop him. They mutually decide to make the return of the Greek ships harder. Upon agreeing his, the two gods exit the stage.

Hecabe rises and starts wailing for her city and the death of so many men, and especially for the death of her husband, king Priam of Troy, as a result of a war caused by an unfaithful woman. A chorus of captured Trojan women comes out of the tents, wondering who their masters will be. They fear they might have to live in hated Helen's country and be ruled by her husband, Menelaus.

Talthybius comes in and announces to the Trojan women how they have been allotted. Hecabe's daughters' fate is that Cassandra, the holy virgin of Phoebus, will accompany Agamemnon as his secret concubine, while

Polyxene will serve at the tomb of Achilles. Andromache, the wife of Hecabe's oldest son, Hector, has been awarded to Neoptolemus while Hecabe has been assigned to Odysseus.

Cassandra comes out of a hut in a state of trance. She prophesies that her nuptials with Agamemnon will bring terrible disasters to his whole family. She also foresees Hecabe's death in Troy and the endless wanderings of Odysseus. Talthybius with his men take Cassandra and leave. Hecabe continues her lament until she collapses exhausted on the ground, where she stays motionless.

A chariot appears with Andromache on. She is holding her son Astyanax in her arms. She gets out of the chariot and tells Hecabe that her daughter Polyxene was slaughtered on Achilles' tomb. She consoles Hecabe by saying that it was better for Polyxene to die than to live. Andromache talks about the only man of her life, Hector. Despite being Hector's mother, Hecabe advises her to forget her dead husband and to honour her new man, Neoptolemus. Only this way she will be able to bring up her son Astyanax, who one day might rebuild Troy.

Talthybius comes in again. After a proposal by Odysseus, they have decided to kill Astyanax, as being Hector's offspring they fear his retaliation in the future. Andromache, completely horrified, takes Astyanax in her arms, but Talthybius advises her to give him the child without resistance, as she would not want her disobedience to irritate the Achaeans, resulting in her child remaining unburied. Andromache, persuaded by his words, hands the child to Talthybius and leaves.

The chorus starts wailing again as they narrate their city's history.

Menelaus appears on the stage and reveals that he plans to execute Helen when they return home. Helen enters, and hearing Menelaus, asks him to let her defend herself. Hecabe intervenes in their conversation, asking to be the persecutor against Helen.

Helen accuses Hecabe of giving birth to Paris, whom fate arranged to be asked to judge three goddesses and to choose the most beautiful amongst them. It was neither Helen's nor Paris' fault that the winner, Aphrodite was to offer Helen as a gift to him. She believes that Menelaus should forgive her and punish Aphrodite instead. Hecabe responds to Helen by saying that it was not Aphrodite who made her do this, on the contrary, she was the one who fell in love with her handsome son. Nor was she forced to leave Sparta. Besides, when Paris died, Hecabe had advised her many times to return to Menelaus, but she preferred Troy's palaces and grandeur. Hecabe recommends to Menelaus not to give any attention to Helen's plea and to sentence her to death. Menelaus agrees and Hecabe advises him to avoid taking the cursed woman on his ship, as she could lure him out of going through with his decision.

Talthybius appears carrying the dead Astyanax in Hector's large shield. He says that he died when the Greeks threw him off the city walls. Hecabe decorates the body and orders the soldiers to bury it. They take the shield containing the body and leave. The chorus starts crying as they see soldiers on the rooftops of the city burning down Troy. Hecabe, lamenting, wants to burn with her city. The soldiers remind her that she now belongs to Odysseus and it is her duty to join him at the Achaean ships. Troy's castle collapses, as soldiers approach to take the women.

The tragedy ends with the chorus crying for the burning city, which will now lose everything, even its name. The sound of the collapsing castle is heard and the Trojan women start walking towards the Achaean ships.

PHILOCTETES
(SOPHOCLES)

On the seashore of Lemnos island near the entrance of a cave, Neoptolemus, the son of hero Achilles, is informed by Odysseus that Philoctetes was abandoned there. It was a decision of the Achaean fleet's leaders, because his leg was wounded by a viper's bite and his cries of pain were annoying them while they were sacrificing to the gods.

Odysseus asks Neoptolemus to help him find Philoctetes' cave. He adds that if Neoptolemus discovers him, he should say to him that the Achaeans had deceived him and that he was angry with them. Neoptolemus proposes to use violence in order to bring Philoctetes to Troy, as cheating is not in his nature. However, Odysseus persuades him by reminding him that Philoctetes is in possession of deadly arrows, the arrows of Heracles which were donated to him by the hero himself at the time of his death. Only by deceiving him they will be able to get the man along with his precious weapons.

The chorus, comprising of the crew of Neoptolemus' ship, is heard declaring their compassion for Philoctetes, who lives alone, suffering from the pains of an incurable wound. Philoctetes arrives, dragging his leg and moaning.

He asks the strangers who they are and what has brought them to the island. Neoptolemus pretends he does not know Philoctetes, who starts narrating his story, speaking against the Achaeans. Neoptolemus agrees with what he says. He mentions how unfair they were to him when they gave Odysseus the weapons and the armour of his father Achilles, which rightfully belonged to him. Philoctetes asks Neoptolemus to take him to Scyros, where Neoptolemus had been intending on traveling. With the chorus assisting his plea, Neoptolemus is eventually persuaded.

A sailor from the crew appears together with a foreign trader. He notifies Neoptolemus that the Achaeans are searching for him in order to bring him back. Odysseus, they add, has gone to bring Philoctetes back to Troy, because the Trojan prophet Helenus has given an oracle that unless they do so, they will never be able to capture Troy. After the departure of the merchant, Neoptolemus and Philoctetes agree to leave immediately before Odysseus arrives. Neoptolemus asks to see the famous arrows and Philoctetes allows him to hold them, something nobody except he and Heracles had ever done. As they are about to enter the cave where the arrows are kept, Philoctetes shouts in pain. He is in the early stages of one of his frequent crises, after which he falls into a deep sleep for many hours. He fears that, as the merchant told them, Odysseus might arrive during his sleep to take his arrows. He entrusts them to Neoptolemus, as he has been persuaded he is an honest man.

Neoptolemus, feeling guilty, reveals the truth to the

wounded man. Philoctetes cannot believe that this polite young man has been deceiving him all along in an attempt to take his arrows, which above all help him hunt down his daily food. Neoptolemus hesitates – should he give back the arrows? Before he can take his final decision, Odysseus returns on stage and tries to persuade Neoptolemus to give the arrows to him instead. He also adds that according to the oracle, together with his weapons, Philoctetes too must be brought back to Troy. Philoctetes threatens to throw himself off the rock into the sea so all would be lost. Odysseus exits, leaving Philoctetes alone with the chorus.

Odysseus and Neoptolemus approach; Neoptolemus has repented and wants to return the weapons. He believes that the way he seized them was indecent and unbecoming to him and that he must make things right. Odysseus threatens him that if he does such a thing, he will have to face the whole Argive army.

Philoctetes comes out of the cave and Neoptolemus gives him the arrows. Odysseus intervenes at once and Philoctetes, armed once more, prepares to kill him. Neoptolemus tries to change his mind by telling him that only if he comes to Troy together with his weapons will the sons of Asclepius heal his wound and allow for Troy to be captured. All this has been foretold by the seer Helenus. Philoctetes is adamant and asks to be taken back to his own country, as was promised to him. Neoptolemus agrees but wonders how he will escape the wrath of the Achaeans. Philoctetes then promises to help him, using the Herculean arrows.

At this point the voice of Heracles is heard from the heavens. Zeus, the father of gods, wants them to act differently. They must go to Troy together, where Philoctetes will be healed and will end up killing Paris with his arrows. As for Neoptolemus, he should know he needs Philoctetes in order for Troy to be captured. The two men promise that they will obey the divine orders.

P H O E N I C I A N   W O M E N
(EURIPIDES)

Jocasta comes out of the palace of Thebes. She recalls Apollo's oracle to her husband Laius that they should not have any children because he was to be killed by a child of theirs. However, he did not show any restraint and a boy was born. Full of fear, Laius gave the baby to some shepherds to abandon to Mount Cithaeron. A servant, however, took the child from the mountain and gave it to his childless masters, Polybus, the king of Corinth, and his wife Merope. The boy, called Oedipus, grew up and heard that his parents had adopted him, so he went to the oracle in order to find out who his biological parents were. On his way there he met Laius, and a misunderstanding led him to kill him, his identity unknown to him. The oracle which he received after the incident ordained that he would kill his parents. In an attempt to avoid this, he decided not to return to Corinth but to go to Thebes instead. On his way there he killed the Sphinx, the horrible monster. As a reward, upon his arrival to Thebes he married Jocasta and became the king of the city. They had four children together: Eteocles, Polynices, Antigone and Ismene. When he discovered the truth he blinded himself. His two sons locked him into the palace and he cursed them to "share his kingdom with a sword". They decided to take turns on the throne, reigning for a year each. Polynices, being the youngest of the two, left the city to allow Eteocles to rule first. But a year later when the time came for Eteocles to hand the throne over to Polynices, Eteocles refused to do so. Polynices meanwhile had married the daughter of the king of Argos, so he gathered an army of Argives and campaigned against Thebes in order to take the throne back.

Jocasta enters the palace as Antigone and the pedagogue are leaving. The pedagogue points to the horizon and shows her the Argive army approaching. Polynices is ready to attack their city; they can discern the seven army leaders, all famous for their bravery. A chorus of Phoenician women enters. They refer to their ancestry and say that they were sent to Thebes, selected as an offering to become god Apollo's slaves in Delphi. Polynices appears and they have a conversation. The chorus says that Polynices has justice on his side, but they fear the city might be destroyed. They call Jocasta to come out of the palace and meet her child.

Jocasta welcomes Polynices, who talks about his wish to resolve the issue in a peaceful way. When Eteocles appears, he tells him that if he honours their initial agreement he will send the army back and give him the throne of Thebes after one year, as they had already agreed. Jocasta begs Eteocles to keep his word. The king, using the weak argument that Polynices had come with an army to request the throne, refuses and explicitly states that he prefers to be unjust than to lose his reign. Jocasta tries to change his mind, but in vain. Eteocles threatens to kill Polynices, who after asking to see his father and sisters, leaves declaring that he will deal with his brother in combat.

Eteocles meets with Creon, his mother's brother and together they plan the city's defense against the enemy attack. In this meeting they also decide to marry Antigone to Haemon, Creon's son. Lastly, Eteocles orders that if Polynices gets killed in the battle his burial is to be forbidden and that anyone who disobeys this order will be condemned to death. Then Eteocles leaves, asking Creon to call Teiresias to obtain an oracle.

The blind seer Teiresias enters the stage supported by his daughter. Along with them comes Menoeceus, another son of Creon. Teiresias is angry with Eteocles and initially refuses to give an oracle to him. Eventually, however, he accepts and asks Menoeceus to leave so he can speak. When they inform him that Menoeceus went away, he says that in order for the people and the city to be saved, Menoeceus must be sacrificed to Ares, the god of war. Teiresias and his daughter leave and Creon orders his son to leave the city at once. Menoeceus pretends to obey and exits, but then reveals to the chorus that he is willing to be sacrificed in order to help his city.

The chorus admires Menoeceus' love for his country as well as his bravery. A herald arrives bringing news from the war and asks to see Jocasta. He tells her about the sacrifice of

Menoeceus and that the outcome of the war was agreed to be decided in a duel between her two sons. He advises Jocasta to run immediately to her children in case her maternal plea changes their mind. Jocasta runs, taking Antigone with her.

Creon appears, holding his dead son Menoeceus in his arms. Another herald comes in and announces that the two brothers have killed each other and that Jocasta committed suicide over their dead bodies. However, the Thebaeans won. Antigone enters, mourning for her dead mother and brothers. She asks the servants to bring her blind father out of the palace. In response to her call, Oedipus comes out and finds out what has happened.

Creon arrives too, announcing that Eteocles has left the throne to Haemon, who will marry Antigone. He sends Oedipus into exile, referring to an oracle by Teiresias which said he brings bad luck to the city. He also announces that, while Eteocles will be buried with royal honours, Polynices will remain unburied. Antigone then decides to bury her brother herself, even if this means she will be sentenced to death. She also declares that she will not accept Haemon as her husband. She decides to leave the city, accompanying her father.

THE LIBATION BEARERS –
ORESTEIA, PART II
(AESCHYLUS)

In Argos, over the tomb of king Agamemnon who was killed by his wife Clytemnestra and her lover Aegisthus, Orestes and his loyal friend Pylades mourn. Orestes has just returned to his country and is bending over the tomb. He cuts some of his hair and leaves it as an offering on the stone, vowing to take revenge for his father's murder.

Slave girls dressed in black form the chorus, which arrives sent by queen Clytemnestra to pour libations on the tomb. They wail for the unjust loss of their king and wait for divine punishment to those who deserve it. Amongst them Orestes recognises his sister Electra and hides so he can observe what they are about to do.

Electra does not know what to say while pouring libations on behalf of the killer and the chorus advises her to ask the gods to send vengeance for her father's death, for blood must be paid for with blood. Electra completes the offering while wailing and talking to her father. In her wailing she stresses the fact that she has been reduced to a slave within her father's palace and that her brother is living in exile. As she touches the tomb, she sees the hair placed on it and notices the footprints around it. The chorus thinks the hair belongs to her lost brother Orestes. Electra does not believe this, but gets upset nonetheless.

Then Orestes appears, reveals his identity to Electra and tells her that he will kill the two lovers who are responsible for his father's murder, himself. God Apollo has given an oracle that, if he does not kill them he would develop leprosy and would also suffer other terrible torments by his father's Furies. The chorus encourages Agamemnon's children, speaking of the ancient law of vengeance and blood, revealing to them that prior to Agamemnon's burial Clytemnestra went as far as to abuse his corpse. Electra and Orestes mourn over the grave, asking for help from their father and from the gods in order to win, while the chorus asks from them to cease wailing and tells them that the time has come to act.

When Orestes asks about the libations being poured, the chorus responds that Clytemnestra has sent them, because the night before she dreamt that she had given birth to a snake. She put the snake on her chest when it started sucking milk from her breast. But as well as milk, the snake was also drinking blood. When Orestes hears of the dream, he says it is clear that the snake represents him and goes to the palace.

There, Orestes and Pylades appear as strangers and Clytemnestra offers them her hospitality. Orestes says he is from Phocis where he met a man called Strophius, who upon hearing he was going to Argos asked him to inform the parents of Orestes that their son had died and they have to decide whether to take his ashes or have them buried in a foreign land. Clytemnestra bursts out in fake wailing over her son's death and she asks Orestes' nurse to go to Aegisthus to tell him to come. The nurse, also wailing, goes out to find Aegisthus. She talks with the head of the chorus who advises her to notify Aegisthus to come alone and without any weapons. The chorus, always helping Orestes, begs the gods to assist him in the execution of his plan.

Aegisthus enters the palace in order to learn more from the strangers about the death of Orestes and as he does so, he is killed. Clytemnestra appears and learns of her lover's death. She mourns Aegisthus in front of Orestes, having realised by then that he is her son. Orestes gets ready to kill her but hesitates hearing her pleas. Pylades reminds him of Apollo's oracles and his oath of revenge and makes him change his mind. Orestes promises his mother a place in the tomb of Aegisthus, whom she loves so much. She begs him but also threatens him that the Furies will hunt him for her death. He responds that even if he does not kill her, the Furies will also chase him, this time for not taking revenge for the death of his father. The chorus speaks about a triumph of justice, which has at last come to this palace which has been disgraced by Agamemnon's murder. The time for the punishment of the sacrilegious has finally come.

Orestes addresses the chorus saying that the events unfolded exactly as the two that lay dead in front of them had predicted: they had vowed to kill Agamemnon together and also die together. After a while, Orestes tells the chorus that he can see the Furies coming, the deities of revenge sent after him by his mother's soul. Fearful, he prays to Apollo to save him and departs.

The tragedy ends with the chorus wondering when this evil madness will come to an end, as this is the third ordeal for the house of Atreides.

CYCLOPS
(EURIPIDES)

In front of the entrance of a huge cave in Etna, Sicily, comes Silenus, the old and ugly leader of the Satyrs who starts talking about himself and his companions. When Hera ordered to have god Dionysus sold as a slave, he and his children, being Dionysus' followers sailed to find him and bring him back. Then a large wave hit them and threw them on this rock, where they live to this day. There inside caves, live Cyclopes, the man-eating one-eyed giants. One of them, Polyphemus, captured them and they have been his slaves and shepherds ever since. Now Silenus is cleaning his master's cave, waiting to welcome him.

A group of Satyrs arrives, forming the drama's chorus, bringing with them the sheep they look after. Silenus announces that he sees a Greek ship approaching, and indeed a short while later the ship's sailors and captain arrive. They carry empty hampers and jugs with them to fill with food and water. They are of course unaware of his master, the man-eating Polyphemus.

Odysseus and his companions arrive; they have been wandering since the end of the Trojan War. Silenus informs them that the place is populated by Cyclopes, who immediately kill and eat any foreigner who happens to pass by. Odysseus asks him where his master is and learns that he has gone hunting. When Silenus asks Odysseus how he will pay for the hospitality and supplies he wants, he answers that he will pay with the wine he has in his magic goatskin, which never runs out. He gives him some to taste and Silenus is delighted. In order to secure some wine for himself, he steals some of his master's animals to exchange them for wine. He tells Odysseus to leave immediately, but at that moment Polyphemus arrives.

He wants to know what is going on, as he does not see Silenus working as he should. Instead of Silenus, the chorus answers, saying that they have carried out all of Silenus' tasks and the only thing they ask for as payment is not to be eaten by him.

Polyphemus enters his cave and sees the foreigners with the supplies Silenus has prepared for Odysseus. He also observes that the face of Silenus is black as if he has been beaten. Silenus says that the foreigners wanted to steal his belongings and he protected them. Polyphemus decides to kill the strangers and eat them. He is particularly happy to do so as he has not had a human meal for quite some time.

Odysseus contradicts Silenus, who takes a vow that he is telling the truth. Polyphemus asks who they are, and it seems that he is aware of the events of the Trojan War. Odysseus tells him that the war was god's will and adds that they are now in need and are standing in front of him as suppliants.

They beg him to spare their lives, but Polyphemus is not interested. He sees them solely as food and pushes Odysseus and his men inside the cave.

A choral part ensues, with the Satyrs accusing Polyphemus and wishing he would disappear together with his cave. They see Odysseus and ask him what has happened. He answers that Polyphemus chose two of his men, roasted and ate them. After that he went to bed and Odysseus gave him some of his wine to taste. Polyphemus liked it very much and started drinking more. Feeling dizzy from the wine, he fell asleep. Then Odysseus tells the chorus about his plan: he will impale a hot stick deep into Polyphemus' only eye in order to blind him. After that he will gather everybody, his crew and the Satyrs and they will all leave this place. The chorus is delighted and all of them agree to participate in the plan.

Odysseus enters the cave again. After a while, he comes out joined by Silenus and Polyphemus. The giant continues to drink the wine, which is now being served to him without any water by Odysseus. He asks Odysseus for his name and Odysseus answers that he is called "Nobody". Drunken, the Polyphemus leaves the others and goes inside the cave together with a horrified Silenus whom Polyphemus has just announced that he desires.

The time for the blinding approaches and all the Satyrs who had earlier agreed to participate start coming up with excuses for their withdrawal. In the end, Odysseus enters the cave alone. A few minutes later Polyphemus' cries can be heard, saying that he has lost his sight.

He appears at the entrance of the cave and says that he has been destroyed by Nobody, as Odysseus had claimed to be called. The Satyrs of the chorus take revenge in their own way, and start mocking him, asking why he is complaining as nobody has destroyed him. Then, they direct him left and right to where his enemy is supposed to be, making him whirl around like a madman.

Odysseus finally comes out and reveals his true name. Polyphemus then remembers an oracle predicting that Odysseus would blind him. He angrily adds that the same oracle predicted that Odysseus would struggle for years in the sea. He threatens that he will throw a rock to crush him, but he has lost his strength and he does not scare Odysseus, who has defeated him, nor the chorus, who depart with Odysseus.

Relevant myths

The Trojan War

When the mortal Peleus married goddess Thetis, they had forgotten to invite the goddess Eris to the wedding. In order to take revenge, Eris threw a golden apple bearing the inscription "to the most beautiful woman" amongst the guests. Soon the three most important of the goddesses present, Athena, Hera and Aphrodite were each claiming the apple for themselves. Zeus, the leader of the gods, chose Paris as a judge, a shepherd and the son of Troy's king Priam. Hera promised Paris that she would make him the king of all Asia and Europe if he chose her. Athena promised him either the kingdom of Phrygia and the destruction of Greece, or to make him the strongest warrior. But Paris chose Aphrodite, who had promised him the most beautiful mortal woman on Earth, Helen. Unfortunately Helen was already married to Menelaus, the king of Sparta. Paris, following Aphrodite's advice, went to Sparta and when Menelaus left for a trip to Crete, he abducted Helen and brought her to Troy. In a variation on the myth, Hera made a replica of Helen and deceived Paris, sending the true Helen to Egypt to be kept chaste by the Egyptian king Proteus, until her husband's return.

Menelaus and his brother Agamemnon, the king of Argos, incite all the Achaeans to gather a large army to go to Troy to bring Helen back. They do this by invoking the oath of Tyndareus: when Helen was about to choose her future husband, her father Tyndareus had forced her numerous suitors, the most eligible Greek princes amongst them, to take an oath that if anyone abducted her in the future they would return her to her husband. But for the army to be carried to Troy, many ships had to depart from Aulis after being stuck there for months due to unfavourable winds. Agamemnon, who had been elected as the general chief of the allied army, was forced to sacrifice his own daughter, Iphigeneia, to the goddess Artemis, whose wrath prevented the ships from sailing. At the last moment, however, Artemis saved Iphigeneia and put a doe in her place to be sacrificed instead.

Troy was besieged for ten years by the Achaeans and was finally captured by deceit. The Greeks made a large wooden horse, subsequently known as the "Trojan Horse" and abandoned it in the fields in front of the city, while they pretended to depart, discouraged, on their ships. The Trojans pulled the horse inside their city and during the night that followed, several of the best Greek warriors who were hidden inside emerged and opened the gates of Troy, using fires to notify their fleet which was hidden behind an islet to come and capture the city.

Helen was the daughter of Zeus, who transformed into a swan had slept with her mother Leda, the wife of Tyndareus. Leda gave birth to an egg, from which Helen and Polydeuces were hatched. Besides Helen, who he considered his own child, Tyndareus had a son, Castor, and another daughter,

Clytemnestra, who married Agamemnon. Helen married Menelaus and they had a daughter, Hermione who according to some sources stayed in Sparta and according to others lived with Clytemnestra when her mother eloped with Paris. Hermione married either Orestes or Neoptolemus, the son of Achilles. In an alternative version, she married Orestes after the murder of Neoptolemus.

Thetis and Peleus, the couple whose wedding was the ultimate reason for the Trojan War, had a heroic child, Achilles, the best warrior the Greeks had in Troy. Achilles was killed by Paris, who hit him with an arrow following an order of god Apollo. The god directed the arrow so that it hit the hero on the ankle, his only weak point. Ajax took his body and, helped by Odysseus, brought it to the Greek camp. After the funeral, his mother Thetis offered the arms of Achilles to the best warrior. They were given to Odysseus who was the most clever and cunning amongst the men, instead of Ajax, who was the bravest.

King Priam of Troy was married to Hecabe. Together they had numerous daughters as well as 19 sons. The most valiant of them was Hector, while the most harmful for Troy was Paris. Indeed due to a prophetic dream his mother had, Paris was left on a mountain as a baby. He managed to escape death however and later was recognised again as a member of the royal family. Polydorus and Helenus the seer are also mentioned in greek tragedies. Helenus as a prisoner of war had predicted that in order to capture Troy the Greeks had to bring Philoctetes with the arrows of Heracles. Of the royal daughters, Cassandra and Polyxene are mentioned.

Apollo, the god of oracle, had been in love with Cassandra and gave her the gift of predicting the future. Afterwards, however, she refused to give herself to him. Unable to take back his own gift, Apollo punished her by cursing her so that nobody ever believed her predictions. She predicted the destruction Paris would bring upon Troy when he was united with his family, the capture of Troy with the use of the Trojan Horse, Agamemnon's murder and even her own death, but in vain.

Polyxene was sacrificed on the tomb of Achilles to honour him, as his ghost had requested. Only this way the Greek ships could set sail for the voyage home. Achilles had seen Polyxene during the war, and according to rumours, he had asked her to become his wife.

Hector was married to Andromache. After his death and the capture of Troy, Andromache was given as a slave to Neoptolemus, the son of dead Achilles.

THE STORY OF ATREIDES

Atreus had a wife called Aerope. She developed an intimate relationship with his brother Thyestes and they stole from Atreus a golden lamb, gifted to him by god Hermes. Atreus had an agreement with the noblemen of the region that the owner of the lamb would be the king of Argos, so as a result he lost his throne. When Zeus, the leader of the gods, learned about this indecent act, he suggested to Atreus to bet that the following day the Sun would rise from the West. If he won, he would be the king of Argos again. Atreus accepted and, through the intervention of Zeus, won the bet. According to one version the adultery was also revealed and Atreus killed his wife, while Thyestes was exiled. In another version Thyestes left, but the adultery was revealed years later. In any case, many years later Atreus invited Thyestes to a dinner in order to show him that everything had been forgotten. But nothing had been forgotten. During the dinner, he served Thyestes his own children, having first killed and cooked them. Thyestes ate them, not suspecting what his meal was and only at the end did Atreus show him their heads. Thyestes cursed Atreus and all his descendants and left. According to one variant, he had one more son, Aegisthus, who entered the service of king Agamemnon.

When Agamemnon, the son of Atreus, left for the Trojan War, Aegisthus, whom Agamemnon had left behind as a viceroy, became involved with his wife Clytemnestra. When Agamemnon returned, they murdered him together with his slave, Cassandra the soothsayer. Clytemnestra's motive was that he had sacrificed their daughter Iphigeneia, and that he had numerous extramarital relations, with Chryseis, one of his slaves during the war, and Cassandra amongst others.

Agamemnon's murder was avenged by his son Orestes, who was incited by an Apollonian oracle and was assisted and encouraged by his sister Electra and his friend and cousin Pylades. After the murder, Orestes was persecuted and tormented by the Furies, primal deities who punish murderers. He was only relieved after being tried at Areios Pagos in Athens, the first ever trial for a murder, where he was acquitted.

HERACLES – IO – DANAIDS

Heracles, the most celebrated Greek hero, was the son of Zeus and Alcmene, but also had a mortal father, Amphitryon, Alcmene's husband. Persecuted by the goddess Hera, the jealous wife of Zeus, he had to serve king Eurystheus of Argos, his cousin who he hated, for twelve years. Eurystheus ordered him to accomplish twelve difficult feats, known as the twelve labours of Heracles. The reason for the subordination of Heracles to Eurystheus is variously cited as either the killing of his family after Hera drove him mad, or as a favour to Amphitryon who had accidentally killed Electryon, Heracles' grandfather. Women were the greatest weakness of Heracles, and he married several of them. In the tragedies two of them are mentioned, Megara and Deianira. Megara was awarded to him by Creon, the king of Thebes, to thank Heracles for relieving the city from a heavy tax it was paying to the Minyan inhabitants of Orchomenos.

Heracles even liberated Theseus, the other great Greek hero and king of Athens. Theseus with his friend Peirithous had visited Hades, the king of the underworld, to abduct Persephone, his wife. Hades welcomed them, but he invited them to sit at the throne of Lethe (oblivion), from which it was impossible to get up. With the permission of Persephone Heracles set Theseus, but not Peirithous, free when he accomplished his twelfth labour, which involved stealing Cerberus, Hades' three-headed dog and guardian of the dead.

According to the myths, the funeral fire of Heracles was ignited by Philoctetes and the hero gave him his arrows as a reward.

Heracles was a descendant of Io, a beautiful maiden and priestess of the goddess Hera, who was loved by Zeus. Io, persecuted by Hera, the jealous wife of Zeus, was transformed into a cow and was chased through many countries by Oestrus, the horsefly Hera sent after her. The Ionian Sea and Bosporus were named after her (Bous meaning ox) to commemorate her passage. Crossing the Caucasus Io met Prometheus, bound on the rock, who prophesised that one of Io's descendants would set him free, as indeed happened. Io finally found rest in Egypt where she was turned into a woman again, but not before giving birth to Epaphus, who was conceived with a mere touch of Zeus' hand. Epaphus was the ancestor of two brothers, Danaus and Aegyptus. The 50 sons of Aegyptus tried to force the 50 daughters of Danaus to marry them, but the girls escaped to Argos, where they found protection from their cousins. After a war, however, they were forced to marry them. In retaliation their father, Danaus, ordered the girls to murder their husbands during the first night of their wedding. All obeyed him except for one, who became the ancestor of Heracles. The remaining 49, according to one myth, were punished after their death to eternally carry water in bottomless earthenware jars.

OEDIPUS

Laius, son of Labdacus, king of Thebes, was exiled as a child when usurpers killed his father and seized the throne. Laius was given refuge by Pelops, the Peloponnesian king. Growing up there he fell in love with the king's son, Chrysippus, who could not stand the shame and committed suicide. Goddess Hera then cursed Laius and his descendants (the house of Labdacidae).

After the death of the usurpers in Thebes, Laius returned there as a king and married Jocasta, Creon's sister. A divine oracle had warned him against having children, as one of them would kill him. Despite this he had one son who he gave away to a shepherd when he was a baby, asking him to abandon him in the mountains. The shepherd, however, felt sorry for the child and gave him up for adoption to the childless royal pair of Corinth, Polybus and Merope. This child was Oedipus. As an adult, Oedipus heard that he was not their biological child and he went to ask the oracle who his real parents were. The oracle he received was that he would kill his father and marry his mother. Horrified, Oedipus decided not to return to Corinth and headed towards Thebes. On his way there, he came across his biological father Laius and after a quarrel Oedipus ended up killing him, being unaware of his identity. Continuing his way, Oedipus met and killed the Sphinx, a monster who asked passers-by to solve a riddle, eating them when they failed. Oedipus solved the riddle and killed the Sphinx. After the death of Laius was announced in Thebes, the prize for the person who would relieve the city from the Sphinx was to marry Jocasta and become the king of Thebes. Thus Oedipus married his mother and became the king. Years later, after having four children with her (Eteocles, Polynices, Antigone and Ismene) a plague broke out in the country. The oracle said that the killer of the previous king should be found and exiled for the city to be relieved from the ordeal. After investigation, the truth was revealed. Jocasta committed suicide and Oedipus blinded himself. His sons did not treat him well, according to different authors he was exiled, imprisoned or simply not defended against Creon. Oedipus cursed them to have to "share his kingdom with a sword". The two brothers decided to take turns to the throne, ruling for a year each. Polynices left the city to let Eteocles to reign first. But a year later when the time came for Eteocles to hand the kingdom over to Polynices, Eteocles refused to do so. Meanwhile Polynices had married the daughter of the Argive king, so he gathered an army of Argives and campaigned against Thebes in order to take the kingdom back. The two brothers ended up killing each other, while Thebes escaped capture by the Argive army. Creon, who seized the throne, prohibited the burial of Polynices. Antigone disobeyed his order and was condemned to live in an underground cell for life and in turn, committed suicide. Other versions of the story say that she followed Oedipus when he was exiled. Together they went to Athens, where Oedipus, now acknowledged by the gods as having been punished unjustly, since his crimes were committed without his knowledge, leaves Earth as a mortal and earns a position amongst the gods.

COMEDIES

ASSEMBLY WOMEN
(ARISTOPHANES)

Before the break of dawn, while it is still dark, Praxagora comes out of her house with great secrecy. She is holding men's clothing and shoes along with a stick and false beard, as if preparing to be disguised as a man. Her monologue explains that she has called women in a secret meeting, where they will be dressed like men so they can participate in the people's Assembly. There they will take decisions with which power will be passed to women. Indeed, women appear dressed like men. Praxagora advises them to rehearse their speeches before going to the Athenian Assembly, in order to be prepared and know how to speak, act and stand while being there.

A woman starts orating, but makes mistakes. Immediately, Praxagora takes the floor and teaches the other women the proper way to speak at the Assembly. She proposes, speaking as a man, that political power should be given to women for being experienced in housekeeping and therefore in a position to order things better. She reminds that women stick to well-tested ways of doing things, with proven results. As mothers, their prime care is to secure the survival of their children. Women agree both with Praxagora's views and the way she presents them; they proclaim her as their leader and they depart.

The chorus comes, consisting of women from Attica, also dressed in men's clothes, who are going to the Assembly in order to support Praxagora. After they have left, Blepyrus appears; he is Praxagora's husband and is dressed with his wife's orange dress. He meets a neighbour and they discover they both woke up and could not find their clothes; somebody had taken them so they had to dress in their wives' clothes. A third man comes in, Chremes, who is returning from the Assembly. He describes to them what happened during the discussion about ways to make the state stand on its feet. The main speaker was an unknown beautiful young person who insisted that women are much more capable of securing money, also claiming that they are more discreet than men. When he proposed to give the power to women, his proposition was voted for by the majority and as a result the administration has passed over to them.

The chorus passes again; they go aside and take off their disguises, assuming again their female form. Praxagora appears, happy from the success of their plan and the women depart for their houses. Before Praxagora reaches her house she runs into Blepyrus. He suspects that she was involved in foul play but she claims that she run out in a hurry to help a friend give birth and as she could not find her clothes, took his to shield herself from the cold. When Blepyrus is relieved from his suspicions, he tells her that the people's

Assembly voted that the women should assume the political power. Praxagora pretends that this is news to her.

However, the chorus appears and asks Praxagora to put her political plans into practice. Indeed, she starts by announcing the new measures and laws on property. There is to be equality in property; with the redistribution of wealth, there will be no rich and poor people. Even for sexual partners there will be equality: Both men and women will have the right to choose, neither of them having the right to exclusivity. A kind of safety valve will exist in order to ease the pressure on the young and beautiful: in order to get to the bed of someone popular, one will have the obligation to satisfy someone less attractive. Praxagora leaves to organise common meals. In the evening the first public feast will be given for all Athenians.

As expected, certain problems are bound to arise. The richest citizens refuse to give up their wealth to be redistributed equally. A young and an old woman appear at the windows of adjacent houses. They quarrel about their appeal and erotic abilities and finally the old woman malevolently makes clear to the young one that whoever wishes to sleep with her, would have to pass from her house first according to the new law. The young woman leaves her window, while a young man appears, asking her to open her door, because he is burning from his desire for her body. However, the old woman comes out of her house and reminds him of the law: before he can be with the young woman, he has to pass from an elder's bed. The man does not obey and rebukes her with offensive words, but the woman starts dragging him. The man tries to resist but finally realises that he must accept his fate. Then the young woman appears and speaks harshly to the old one, telling her that it is impossible to compel such a young man to go with a woman at his mother's age. The old woman retreats, but before the young couple have the time to enter the house of the maiden, another old woman appears and starts pulling the young man, not leaving him before he accomplishes with her his legal duty to those advanced in age. After a while a third elderly woman, more dynamic than the first two, comes to claim him. The young man turns to the audience: how will he manage to accomplish such a feat? All except the chorus exit the stage.

Soon, Praxagora's servant arrives announcing that everybody is happy. Blepyrus appears and the servant tells him that she has come ordered by her lady to lead him to the feast; there is plenty of food and good wine to eat and drink. The comedy ends with everybody being led, singing and dancing, to the feast that has been prepared for them.

LYSISTRATA
(ARISTOPHANES)

Lysistrata is waiting for the women she has called for a meeting. The first to appear is Calonice, her neighbour. Talking with her, Lysistrata makes obvious that she is annoyed with the other women for being late for such an important meeting. She says that, if women from all regions of Greece –Boeotia, Peloponnese and Athens– decide to act united, they will save Greece from war. Calonice wonders if this could be true while more women approach, amongst them Lampito from Sparta.

Lysistrata asks the women if they miss their husbands. Everyone's answer is positive: they all miss them and they would like to have peace in order to be able to enjoy them, as war takes them away from their families. Lysistrata quickly puts her idea on the table: when they meet their husbands, they will practice abstinence from sex. Men will be able to enjoy them only if they end the war and make peace.

While initially eager to participate in the peace effort, when the women hear about abstinence, they start voicing excuses and various practical problems that could arise from the application of this plan. However, Lysistrata has also thought of the solution. If they are forced to sleep with their husbands, they can do so without showing willingness. This attitude will leave men unsatisfied. Lampito the Spartan says that as long as Athenians have money to fund it, they will not end the war. Lysistrata reveals that she has already foreseen this problem and she has sent the older women to capture the Acropolis, where public money is kept. The comedy has a double chorus, comprising of men and women. The female part of the chorus comprises of the old ladies who have been sent to the Acropolis. Lampito is the first to accept for the sake of peace. She is followed by the other women; they take an oath over a jug of red wine. Lampito departs for Sparta, while Lysistrata keeps the other foreign women as hostages. She orders them to run to the Acropolis all together and put the bars that lock its entrance gates, so that no man can enter. They do as she orders.

A group of elderly men arrive at the entrance of the Acropolis – they are the male chorus of the comedy. They request the removal of the bars and ask for permission to enter. If the women refuse, they threaten to beat them with the sticks they hold and set them on fire. When they light the fire, a group of women start pouring buckets of water over them. The men, aided by Scythian guardians who have arrived with a magistrate to deal with the situation, decide to force open the gates using levers. During that time Lysistrata had joined the women in the Acropolis to assist in their resistance. When the men are trying to come up with ways to arrest her, a battle between men and women starts as more young women are arriving to the Acropolis. The women win and enter the Acropolis, except for Lysistrata who stays outside along with Calonice and Myrrhine.

The magistrate asks them why they occupied the Acropolis; Lysistrata answers that they did it to guard the city's money, so that men can no longer use it towards the war. From now on the money will be managed by them, as they have the necessary experience from managing their family finances. Women, she adds, suffer twice as much as men in any war, as they bid farewell to their sons and age without their husbands. She stops her oration in order to ridicule the magistrate, who leaves full of indignation to complain to the other magistrates.

In the meantime, some women start craving sex and try to escape using ridiculous excuses. Lysistrata manages to bring them back with the power of her persuasion. After a while Kinesias, Myrrhine's husband, arrives full of desire and tries to persuade her to go with him using various pretexts. Myrrhine, however, flatly refuses: he should not expect her to agree to what he's asking if they do not end the war. Kinesias insists and starts begging her. She pretends to be yielding, but finally goes away, leaving him with his desire unsatisfied, and never appears again.

A herald comes, sent by the Spartans. He meets the Athenian magistrate and tells him that Lampito and the other wives are not letting the men lay a hand upon them if they do not cease the war first. Their quenchless desire is now unbearable and they are forced to ask for conciliation with all Greek cities. The magistrate, who is having the same experience, agrees.

Lysistrata comes down from the Acropolis. She meets with both Athenian and Spartan delegates, all in a priapic state. A beautiful maiden appears as the personification of Conciliation. Lysistrata addresses the Spartans first, then the Athenians. She wisely attributes the part of responsibility for the war that corresponds to each side. Both sides are listening to her, but not with too much attention, as they are distracted by the natural beauty of Conciliation. After the speech, negotiations begin and the delegates ask for various regions with phrases full of sexual innuendoes. Lysistrata intervenes as a mediator. Finally things are going the right way. Wishes can be heard from both sides, wishes that the peace they agreed upon stays with them forever. As they depart, Spartans and Athenians are dancing together, glorifying the gods.

PEACE
(ARISTOPHANES)

This comedy begins in front of the house of Trygaeus in Athens and continues in mount Olympus, the abode of gods. Two servants are on the stage. One suffers from the stench of the manure balls he is making, which are carried by the other servant into a stable situated at the back of the stage, to be eaten by an oversize winged beetle brought there by their master the previous day. Their master, Trygaeus, is seized by madness; he spends his day staring at the sky, shouting at Zeus that he is destroying Greece and trying to come up with ways to visit him.

Trygaeus appears riding the beetle. He explains that the aim of his trip is to visit Zeus and ask him what his plans are concerning the Greeks, who continuously make war against each other. The daughters of Trygaeus come out of the house and implore him not to make this dangerous journey. Trygaeus replies that if his trip is unsuccessful they will not have food to eat. He chose the beetle because, according to the myths it is the only flying being except Pegasus that has managed to reach Zeus; it is also practical because it consumes manure, so he only needs to take food for himself and the beetle's food he will produce.

Indeed, Trygaeus flies a large distance on his beetle and reaches the palace of Zeus, on Mount Olympus. God Hermes, the herald of the gods, opens the door and irritated by the stench, asks him for his name and the reason of his visit. Trygaeus flatters him; he then tells Hermes that he has come to bring him meat and the god softens his attitude. He informs Trygaeus that the gods have ascended high in heavens, because they do not want to see humans at war with each other, or to have to listen to their pleas. Many times they had tried to persuade the Greeks to agree on a peace treaty, but each time it was refused either by the Athenians or by the Spartans. So they left War back on Olympus, telling him to do whatever he wished with the human race. War threw Peace into a deep cave and had its entrance closed with stones, so that the humans would not find it. The previous day, War took a huge mortar and pestle to pulverise the Greeks.

War comes out of the palace and Trygaeus hides himself. War is holding the mortar in his hands and is throwing various materials, each characteristic of a different city. He asks his slave Tarachos for the pestle but Tarachos cannot find it, so they both enter the palace to make one.

Trygaeus comes out of his hiding place, calling peasants, artisans and merchants from all over Greece to get Peace out of her cave, before War has time to construct his pestle. The chorus appears, and ignoring Trygaeus' admonitions, start an endless dance to celebrate the end of war and the joys of peace, proclaiming Trygaeus their leader.

Hermes comes out and threatens them with death if they set Peace free. Trygaeus reminds him of the meat he has brought from earth for him, makes his services available to him and offers him a golden cup. Hermes yields and leads them to the place Peace is imprisoned.

They pull Peace up with ropes; the Athenians and Spartans of the chorus pull the rope with their full power, while the Argives (Argos was a neutral city in the war) pull reluctantly and the Megarians almost without using any force as they are exhausted by hunger. Finally, it is decided that the peasants will do the job better if they are left alone, and they are the ones who eventually bring Peace to the surface.

Two young females are retrieved along with Peace: Opora, the personification of the fruit-bearing land, and Theoria, the personification of official delegations to festivals of friendly cities. The head of the chorus asks why Peace had left Greece. Hermes gives the answer: in the beginning, Pericles produced a resolution excluding the Megarian products from the Athenian market (Megara was an ally of Sparta). After that, the cities allied to Athens bribed the Spartans to start the war, in order to avoid excessive money contributions to Athens.

Hermes orders that Opora should be given to Trygaeus as his wife, while Theoria should be given to the Assembly. As the beetle of Trygaeus has been taken by Zeus to carry his thunders, Trygaeus descends to the earth without it, bringing with him Peace, Opora and Theoria.

Trygaeus orders his servant to prepare Opora as a bride for the wedding, while he goes to the Assembly to give Theoria to one of the city officials. The chorus hails Trygaeus as their saviour and he decides that an official inauguration of Peace must take place where he will sacrifice a lamb, the most peaceful animal. They light the sacrificial fire and the servant comes in, holding in his hands two pieces of meat which they place on it. Hierocles the soothsayer appears, curious of what is going on. When he learns that the sacrifice is in the honour of Peace he opposes it, mentioning prophesies to persuade them that the time for peace has not come yet. Trygaeus insists and Hierocles, defeated, merely begs to be given a piece of the sacrificed animal. When Trygaeus refuses, Hierocles tries to steal a piece and is eventually driven away naked and beaten. Trygaeus and his slave enter the house; the chorus express their repugnance to war and glorify peace and the happiness it offers.

Two sellers of sickles and buckets come to offer Trygaeus rich gifts for his wedding, as their business had prospered since he brought Peace on earth. On the other side, a group of weapon merchants come and complain of the fall in their sales, but leave annoyed by the mocking of Trygaeus.

The bride comes out and the wedding ceremony starts. Slaves appear carrying wedding cakes; Wishes in verse form follow and then Trygaeus takes Opora and goes to his fields. The comedy ends with Trygaeus promising cakes to everybody who will follow them.

THE ACHARNIANS
(ARISTOPHANES)

In Pnyx, the hill near the Acropolis of Athens where the citizens gather for their assemblies, Dikaeopolis is complaining that the Athenians are slow to arrive as he wants to propose for discussion the issue of peace with the Spartans. Eventually people start to appear. The first person who tries to speak at the assembly is the immortal Amphitheus, who says he was ordered by the gods to sign a peace treaty with the Spartans. Scythian guards come and drive him away even though Dikaeopolis tries to defend him.

City delegates who have been travelling to seek help with the war arrive. They have already visited Persia to look for gold and Thrace to ask for soldiers and have just returned from their mission. Dikaeopolis criticises them because in his opinion they squander public money when they are on a mission of national importance. A man called Pseudartabas appears. He barely speaks Greek. He presents himself as a delegate of the Persian king, carrying a promise of financial assistance (in gold) from the ruler. Dikaeopolis, however, interrogates him and reveals that he is an Athenian in disguise. He drives him away and finds Amphitheus, gives

171

him the necessary money and sends him to Sparta in order to negotiate a personal peace treaty on his behalf. Amphitheus departs. Immediately after that, Theorus presents the soldiers he returned with from his mission to Thrace and requests a salary for them. One of them grabs a bag with garlic from Dikaeopolis; Dikaeopolis calls them thieves and asks from the assembly to agree not to give them a salary.

It starts drizzling and the public crier announces the end of the assembly. All Athenians leave except Dikaeopolis. A while later Amphitheus returns from Sparta, chased by angry citizens from the demos of Acharnae; these *Acharnians* are blaming him for making peace with the Spartans who had destroyed their fields. Amphitheus meets Dikaeopolis and tells him that he has brought him three kinds of peace treaties, inside three pots. The smallest pot contains a five-year treaty, the middle-sized one a ten-year treaty and the largest pot a thirty-year treaty. Dikaeopolis tries all three and rejects the two shorter treaties, choosing the thirty-year one, which, as he says, smells sweetly of ambrosia and nectar.

The two men leave and the chorus appears, consisting of Acharnian elders who seek to stone the person who made peace with their enemies. While the head of the chorus prompts everyone to that end, Dikaeopolis appears along with his wife, daughter and two slaves who perform a ritual of sacrifice to god Dionysus. As Dikaeopolis speaks triumphantly about the peace he agreed with the Spartans, he is recognised by the Acharnians and attacked.

He tries to placate them, proposing to stand next to

a butcher's block and to be beheaded upon it if he is not successful in persuading them. The Acharnians keep threatening him, so Dikaeopolis grabs a sack and says that in it he holds hostage some of their fellow citizens who he will slay with a knife. The Acharnians then agree to listen to him. Dikaeopolis brings the wooden block, but before he starts his speech he passes by the house of the tragic poet Euripides, well known for the rags with which he dresses his heroes. He begs him and manages to take from him the rags of hero Telephus. He finds this tragedy appropriate as in it Telephus had delivered a speech against the Trojan War and he too had to resort to threatening to kill a child in order to be heard.

Dikaeopolis returns to his block and starts his speech. He believes that the Spartans are not the only ones responsible for the war. Some mindless drunkards abducted a prostitute from the city of Megara. The Megarians snatched two Athenian whores in retaliation. Then the Athenians prohibited the selling of Megarian products in their market, a decision they did not change when the Spartans, allies of Megara, demanded it. This is why the war broke out: "For three whores!" The chorus divide in two semi-choruses, for and against Dikaeopolis.

Those against him call Lamachus, an officer of the Athenian army, for help. Dikaeopolis jeers at Lamachus' uniform and accuses him of receiving a salary while acting like an emissary, leaving others to fight the wars. Lamachus counters by shouting that he will never stop fighting against the Peloponnesians. Dikaeopolis then says that he will start commercial relations with the Peloponnesians, the Megarians and the Boeotians. As they leave, the chorus head informs us that Dikaeopolis won the debate with Lamachus and that the people were persuaded that the decision for the treaty was the right one.

Dikaeopolis draws borders outside his house, defining his marketplace where merchants from all cities are free to enter, while informers and slanderers are excluded. A man from Megara appears with his two daughters. As they are very hungry, the man agrees with the girls to sell them, disguised as pigs. Dikaeopolis decides to buy the two human pigs in exchange for garlic and salt. An informer comes and informs against the Megarian. Dikaeopolis drives him away and enters his house with the girls.

After a while a Boeotian man appears carrying goods. Dikaeopolis buys an eel from him, proposing to pay for it with a unique Athenian product: an informer. The Boeotian agrees as he can make money by showing him at festivals instead of a monkey. Nikarchus, the famous informer, approaches. He is arrested, packed up, and given to the Boeotian man who takes the package and leaves.

A herald appears and announces that whoever empties his wine cup at the wine festival first will earn a skin bag full of wine as a prize. Dikaeopolis can be heard as he prepares himself for the festival. All admire him for the goods he has in his house and ask him to give them a drop of his peace, like a sort of medicine. A best man asks for some to give to the new groom. Dikaeopolis refuses; however, he gives a little peace to the bridesmaid to offer to the bride, since, being a woman, she bears no responsibility for the war.

A herald brings an order to Lamachus to stand guard to the city's entrances in order to prevent the Boeotians from entering. Another herald arrives on behalf of the priest of Dionysus and calls Dikaeopolis for the festival. Lamachus orders his servant to prepare his military knapsack, while Dikaeopolis tells his slave to prepare him a basket for the festival.

A choral ensues and immediately after, the servant of Lamachus appears announcing that his master fell as he tried to jump over a ditch. Soon, Lamachus arrives in bad state. Not knowing what his servant has announced, he says that he was wounded by an enemy weapon. Dikaeopolis returns from the festival embraced by two girls, drunk and full of happiness. The comedy ends with the triumph of Dikaeopolis who won the drinking contest and received the first prize.

THE ARBITRATION
(MENANDER)

Two houses, that of Chairestratos and that of his friend Charisios, frame the stage. Onesimos, Charisios' slave, arrives with a cook. The cook asks the slave why his master, who has just got married, took a flute-player as his concubine. The slave answers that his master was away in a long journey, when five months after the wedding his wife Pamphile gave birth to a baby which was not his. Pamphile gave the child to her old trusted slave, Sophrone, to get rid of. When Charisios returned, Onesimos, afraid for his position in case his master learned of that event, told him everything. Charisios then left his marital home and was living in the adjacent house of a friend. There, trying to forget, he has taken the flute-player Habrotonon to keep him company.

Smikrines, Charisios' father-in-law arrives grumbling about his son-in-law who is wasting away his daughter's dowry and is sleeping away from home. He must give the dowry back. His monologue is overheard by Chairestratos and Habrotonon, who at once go to inform Charisios.

After a talk with his daughter, who tells him she does not want to leave her husband, Smikrines is approached by

Daos, a slave shepherd, and Syriscus, a slave of Chairestratos, accompanied by his wife who is carrying a baby. They are arguing and ask Smikrines to arbitrate their dispute; he accepts. Daos narrates that he found a baby wearing ornaments in the grove he was shepherding his sheep. He took the baby with him, but started having afterthoughts due to the expenses it would incur. The following day he told Syriscus about the baby. Syriscus started begging him to give the baby to him, to replace his own who had recently died. He took the child, but now is asking for the accompanying ornaments. Daos considers this utterly unfair. Syriscus argues that he wants the ornaments for the child, as they will most probably assist in the discovery of the baby's parents. Smikrines decides that the ornaments should indeed be given to the child, and his decision is respected. As Syriscus and his wife examine the ornaments, Onesimos, who happened to be passing by, notices a copper ring. He grabs it, shouting that it is the ring of his master's, which he had lost when he was drunk. Syriscus becomes angry and tries to get it back, but eventually agrees to wait until the following day so that Onesimos can show the ring to his master.

In the next act, Onesimos hesitates to show the ring; its discovery might bring new troubles. Habrotonon comes out complaining that although Charisios pays for her company, he does not want her by his side. Syriscus comes asking Onesimos for the ring, as the one day they had agreed has almost passed. Onesimos explains to him that he is certain that the ring belongs to his master, but is afraid to show it to him. He had lost it during the Tauropolia festival, where he apparently raped and impregnated a maiden, who was forced to expose the baby along with the ring. If he could find the maiden everything would be clear and he could talk to Charisios. But how could he face his master armed only with suspicions? Syriscus states that this is his own problem and leaves.

As Syriscus leaves, Habrotonon approaches Onesimos and tells him that she happened to hear an identical story. The previous year a company of rich girls had hired her to accompany them and play music for them at the festival of Tavropolia. One of the girls went for a walk alone and when she returned she told everyone that she had been raped. She exhorts Onesimos to show the ring to his master, yet he still hesitates, wanting to locate the girl first. Habrotonon on the contrary proposes that they should first establish whether Charisios was indeed the rapist. It could be that Charisios lost the ring in a game of dice or gave it as a pawn. Habrotonon decides to wear the ring herself and pretend that what happened in the festival had happened to her. Certainly Charisios would give himself away in the conversation, and knowing the father would make it easier to search for the mother. Onesimos congratulates her for her idea, adding that if his master believes that Habrotonon is the mother of his child, he might free her (she was a kind of slave). But after Habrotonon has left, Onesimos has a thought: if the mother of the baby is found, then most probably his master will divorce Pamphile and marry the girl he had raped.

Habrotonon succeeds in her plan and it is revealed that Charisios is the father of the child. Smikrines comes, hears this and runs to the house of Charisios to take his daughter back from that prodigal. Pamphile comes out of the house with her father still trying to persuade her to follow him, saying that her husband will now bring Habrotonon to stay with them in the same house and that the concubine will manage to outflank her, making her life unbearable. But Pamphile strongly defends her marriage: Even if Charisios tells her to leave the house, in time he will acknowledge her love for him. So Smikrines leaves empty-handed, as we see Habrotonon coming out of the other house holding the baby. Habrotonon sees Pamphile for the first time and recognises her immediately: She is the maiden who was raped during Tavropolia. She reveals to her that she lied about being the mother of the baby, as this is obviously the child of Pamphile and Charisios. They enter the house of Charisios, as Onesimos is coming out of Chairestratos' house. Onesimos speaks about his master, who has been secretly eavesdropping on the conversation between his father-in-law and Pamphile and was moved by her defence of her marriage and the love she showed for her husband. Full of remorse, he blames himself for not forgiving her, while he too was proven to have fathered an illegitimate son. Soon Charisios himself appears on the stage, having decided to keep his wife, irrespective of what his father-in-law wants. As he talks, Onesimos and Habrotonon arrive, the latter revealing to him that she is not the mother of his child, but unknowingly to him, the mother is his wife Pamphile. Charisios is surprised, but understands everything; happy as can be, he enters his house to reconcile with his wife.

Smikrines returns once again, this time with Sophrone, Pamphile's old slave, to take his daughter by force before her husband wastes her entire dowry. He meets Onesimos who informs him that the pair have reconciled and if he enters the house he will also be able to see his grandchild. Smikrines thinks Onesimos is joking, but the slave continues: had he been so careless with his unmarried daughter that she gave birth to a child five months after her wedding? In the Tauropolia festival his master grabbed a girl and this was the result. But now they had recognised each other and everything was fine. Besides, Sophrone knew about the baby. Smikrines explodes, calling the old woman "a go-between". He is eventually reconciled with Charisios and everything ends with the usual feast.

THE BIRDS
(ARISTOPHANES)

In a country landscape, Pisthetairos and Euelpides, each holding a bird, are searching for Tereus, a man who according to the myth became a hoopoe. They have bought the birds in order to show them the way, but on the contrary they are completely disorientated. Euelpides says that he seeks another country to live in order to avoid the fines imposed in Athens, where the citizens end up in court all the time. So they search for Tereus to ask him if he has seen a better city while flying high in the sky. From a cluster of trees a bird springs forward; this bird is the servant of Tereus, who was transformed into a bird along with his master, so that he would continue to serve him. On the request of the two friends, he wakes his master up. When they meet, the Athenians ask him to suggest a peaceful city, where they can live without fuss, trials and creditors chasing them; Tereus suggests some cities but they reject them. Finally, Pisthetairos proposes that the birds should establish a country of their own, reserving for that purpose the space between the Earth and the Sky.

Tereus calls the other birds to listen to the news. Soon, a

whole flock of birds gathers, forming the comedy's chorus. The head of the chorus, full of distrust and anger towards humans, calls on the birds to arrest them. But Tereus calms them down and Pisthetairos flatters them by telling them they existed before the Earth and the gods were born, and as the first-born children of the Creation they have exclusive rights to its throne. When the birds hear these words, they are moved so much that they proclaim him their governor. Pisthetairos advises them to establish their own city-state by encircling the air space between the Earth and the Sky with a wall. After that, they should question Zeus' authority over them and, if Zeus refuses to grant them independence, they should launch a holy war against him. They should also communicate to the human species that they are now the rulers and request from humans that they sacrifice first to them and then to the gods. If they refuse, the birds will eat all the seeds from their fields and gouge out the eyes of their animals. If they agree, the birds will systematically exterminate the locusts and other insects, while with their ability to tell the future they will share with them their predictions for prosperity. The birds are delighted by his speech and ask him to lead them.

Tereus advises the two friends to eat a root of a certain tree in order to acquire wings like the birds. The wife of Tereus, a flute-player in the form of a nightingale, appears and entertains everybody with the sweet sound of her flute. Both Athenians express their admiration and depart together with Tereus, while the flute-player stays alone with the chorus.

The head of the chorus recalls that, in reality, their genre sprang out of the union of Eros and Chaos, before the birth of the immortals. For some time he keeps mentioning how important the birds are: they help people in love win the hearts of their loved ones, as they use them as gifts; they indicate the succession of the seasons with their migrations, while with the way they fly they provide oracles to the soothsayers.

Pisthetairos and Euelpides appear again, this time with wings on their backs. They start proposing names for the new city and they finally agree on the name *Nephelococcygia* ("Cloud-cuckoo-town"), which sound both light and at the same time majestic. Pisthetairos sends Euelpides to help with the construction of the city's walls and to send two heralds, one to the gods and the other to the humans. He himself will sacrifice a billy-goat to the new gods. Euelpides obeys and leaves grumbling. Pisthetairos leaves too, and returns for the sacrifice. The priest begins the ritual by invoking various birds as gods, but he mentions so many names that Pisthetairos quickly gets bored and drives him away. After a while, a poet dressed in rags appears; he is the composer of hymns written especially for the new city-state. Pisthetairos gives him the cloak of one of the slaves and expels him too. Then a soothsayer arrives bringing an oracle for the new city: if he wants to have good luck, Pisthetairos has to offer various gifts to him. Pisthetairos invokes another oracle, telling him that he must beat him and drives him away violently. After that, he also expels a city planner who wants to design the city plan, a colony inspector and a promoter of laws that favour the Athenians. All of them are driven away because he realises they are hypocrites whose only interest is personal gain. He decides to take his assistants and continue the goat sacrifice that has been interrupted so many times.

A herald comes and announces that the construction of the city's impenetrable walls has been completed and guards have been installed along the walls' length. However, a second herald reports that some god has entered secretly inside the new city. All birds must be prepared to defend it.

Iris, the goddess who serves as the herald of the gods, appears on the air. Pisthetairos interrogates her, adding that she should had acquired permission before entering; the penalty for this is death. She replies that she is coming from Olympus, the abode of the gods, that she is immortal and that Zeus has sent her to tell humans to offer sacrifices to the gods. Pisthetairos counters that the birds have now replaced the gods, so humans have to sacrifice to them. Iris, angered by his impudence, threatens that Zeus will punish him. He replies that he will instead send eagles to burn the palace of Zeus down; as for herself, he will spread her legs open and... Iris leaves, after threatening him once again.

The herald who was sent to the humans by the birds returns tired. When he meets Pisthetairos, he tells him that all humans honour him for his wisdom and they are sending him a golden wreath, acknowledging that he established a celestial city worthy of admiration. Birds have become very popular and they will have many human visitors. Indeed, some of them appear a few minutes later.

First comes a young man who wants to kill his father and take his fortune; he has heard that the birds choke their father. Pisthetairos offers as a counter-example the storks who bring food and feed their old fathers. Instead of wings and a beak that the young man had asked for, he gives him a shield and a helmet. He persuades him to go and fight, so that with his salary he is able to make a living both for him and his father.

After the young man has left, a poet singing out of tune arrives and asks for wings and the voice of a nightingale. Pisthetairos has to chase him in order to close his mouth. The poet leaves, declaring that despite being unsuccessful he will never stop trying to acquire wings to fly.

After him, an informer arrives. He too asks for wings in order to be able to move fast between the two sides of a court, thus earning double money. Pisthetairos beats him and drives him away. He then enters the cluster of trees and only the chorus stays on stage.

Pisthetairos comes out again when Titan Prometheus arrives secretly. The gods are hungry on Olympus, as humans are no longer offering sacrifices. Trivalloi, the barbaric gods, are threatening to attack Zeus with an army if he does not settle the issue. The gods are about to send delegates with conciliatory proposals; however, Prometheus advises the birds to ask for the sceptre of world leadership and Pisthetairos to ask for Vassileia (Sovereignty), a beautiful maiden, to be his wife. Vassileia is responsible for overseeing the thunders of Zeus, but also for all issues of divine government.

The delegates of the gods arrive soon, comprising the hero and demigod Hercules, Poseidon and Trivallos. Pisthetairos appears together with slaves who carry a table with kitchenware with birds-traitors on it, which are killed, plucked and ready to be cooked.

Poseidon offers peace. Pisthetairos sets as as a condition the return of the sceptre of world leadership to the birds. When the gods agree to this, he also asks for Vassileia to be his wife. Poseidon is quick to refuse, but Hercules, being a slave of his own gluttony, asks him to reconsider. Poseidon warns him of the dangers he could face, of losing the inheritance he would surely receive being the son of Zeus if everything comes under the control of the birds. Pisthetairos intervenes, telling Hercules that as an illegitimate child of the king of gods he would not be liable to receive any inheritance in any case. Eventually, in spite of Poseidon's disagreement, the delegation-committee decide by majority to accept the conditions and Pisthetairos departs with them high for the skies to meet Vassileia.

Later a herald announces that the leader approaches holding the beautiful Vassileia, who in turn is holding one of Zeus' thunders in her hands. The head of the chorus call everybody to form a row to welcome the bride and groom with wedding songs. The comedy ends with the pair leaving while dancing, followed by a dancing chorus.

THE CLOUDS
(ARISTOPHANES)

Two houses, the house of the philosopher Socrates and that of Strepsiades, frame the stage. Strepsiades, his son Pheidippides and two servants lie down on mattresses. Strepsiades is speaking out loud, complaining of the debts his son has burdened him with due to his expenses on horses and horse races. Suddenly, he has a great idea. He wakes his son up and urges him to be trained under his neighbour, Socrates, so that he will become a competent orator and, by learning how to prove a wrong case right, get his father out of having to pay his debts. Pheidippides refuses and his angry father asks him to leave the house.

Despite being old and forgetful Strepsiades decides to take lessons himself. He meets Socrates and asks him to teach the "unjust reason" to him, swearing on the gods that he will pay him as much as he wants. Socrates declares that the oaths to the gods are useless, as he and his students honour the deities of Clouds, goddesses of lightning and thunder, which he is now invoking. The Clouds appear, as the chorus of the comedy, and Strepsiades asks them to make him a great orator, so that he can win any trial. The deities promise him to do that.

The lessons with Socrates begin, however the old man is not able to follow the content. Eventually, Socrates dismisses him and Strepsiades, advised by the Clouds, persuades his son to be educated in his place. When Pheidippides finally goes to Socrates, the issue arises of which one of the two "Reasons" will train him: the Just or the Unjust one? They both present themselves and start quarrelling, trying to win over the student. The Just Reason speaks of the ancient education of the children, of the hard training, the modesty and seriousness. Criticising what the Just Reason presented, the Unjust Reason labels them as obsolete and outdated principles. The Just Reason continues dauntlessly, telling Pheidippides that with him he will learn to respect his parents and the elderly. He will also learn to avoid the traps that immoral women may set for him. The women of the chorus express their admiration for the first speaker and tell the Unjust Reason to use other stronger arguments if he wants to persuade Pheidippides.

The Unjust Reason states that nobody has seen any good from morality. When one is moral, one misses out on the fun side of life, the women, the laughter, the food, the wreaths, which makes one's life worthless. With him, Pheidippides will live an immoral life and he will be able, armed with an orator's skills, to slip away and stay unpunished. At the end, the Unjust Reason even manages to win over the Just Reason by making him admit that the tragic poets, the demagogues, and even the majority of the people in the audience of the theatre, follow his principles. Strepsiades decides that the Unjust Reason is the most suitable to tutor his son.

A few months later, Socrates announces to the old man that his son's training has been completed. With his abilities in knavery, he will now be able to evade all accusations, even if there are witnesses against him. In a conversation that follows between father and son, Strepsiades speaks of his fears about the day of the month (expressed in terms of the old and the new moon) in which creditors pay a deposit in order to lodge a complaint against their debtors who have not paid them off in time. His son calms him, saying that a given day cannot be the day of both the old and the new moon at the same time. What the legislator meant was that if a debtor did not pay his debts up to the day of the old moon, his creditor should lodge a complaint against him on the day of the new moon. The authorities have since misinterpreted the law in order to get the money earlier, so he has the right not to accept it. The father is delighted and expresses his admiration for his son – and for himself, for being his father.

Soon, one of Strepsiades' creditors arrives together with a witness, threatening him that he will lodge a complaint against him on the day "of the old and the new moon". Strepsiades invokes everybody to be a witness of the creditor saying that he will file a complaint against him on two different days and then refuses that he owes money to him, agreeing to swear for that to the gods he no longer believes in. Another creditor comes, to whom his son Pheidippides owes money and he speaks of the additional interest that must be paid. Strepsiades, uses a ridiculous sophistry and asks that if the sea does not expand when so many rivers pour their water to it, how then is it possible that interest can increase someone's debt? He refuses that he has an obligation to pay any interest and drives him away. As Strepsiades enters his house, the chorus accuses him of indecency and predict that he will soon feel sorry for his son and his sophistries.

Indeed, after a while Strepsiades comes out of his house unhappy; Pheidippides is chasing him to beat him because in the middle of their dinner they argued upon who is the greatest poet. The old man prefers Aeschylus, considering his son's favourite, Euripides, immoral. Strepsiades insists that it is unacceptable to be beaten by his own child, who was raised by him with such care and toil. In reply, Pheidippides stresses the argument that, as his father was beating him as a child claiming he loved him, he too must now beat his father out of love. Then Strepsiades invokes the laws: there is no law permitting the beating of a father by his son. The son replies that, as the law has been written by a mortal person, and he himself is also mortal, he has the right to change it. He even threatens to beat his mother too.

Strepsiades cannot bear the thought of what his son has just said. He accuses the Clouds for being responsible for what has happened to his son. They reply that when they see people being prone to indecent acts they always let them carry them out in order to experience the fear of gods. Strepsiades admits that it was not right to refuse to pay off his loans. Then he urges his son to come with him to destroy Socrates for giving people lessons of indecency; he adds that this act will be an act of respect towards Zeus. Pheidippides says that these are old-fashioned ideas, as Zeus does not exist and leaves.

Strepsiades is determined to punish Socrates. He orders his servant to demolish the study room, while at the same time he burns it with a torch. When a choked Socrates comes out and asks what is going on, Strepsiades answers that he is punishing him for his impiety to doubt the gods. The chorus exit and the comedy ends.

THE CURMUDGEON
(MENANDER)

The god Pan comes out of a cave, which is a sanctuary of the Nymphs. He speaks about Knemon, a peevish and quarrelsome neighbour. Knemon had married a widow who already had a boy named Gorgias from her first marriage. Knemon had one daughter, Myrrhine, with the widow. However, he was constantly arguing with his wife so she left him and went to live with her son, who lived poorly, cultivating with his slave a small field nearby. Old Knemon lives with his daughter and an old servant, Simike. He is hostile to everybody and works all day, digging and carrying wood. Myrrhine has now come of age and she shows great respect for the Nymphs. Pan appreciates her behaviour and has led a wealthy young man who has come to hunt in the area, Sostratus, to meet and fall in love with her.

Pan exits the stage and Sostratus appears with his friend Chaireas, who has come to assist him with his plans regarding the woman he is in love with. Sostratus has already sent his slave, Pyrrhias, to find Knemon and speak to him about this issue. Pyrrhias appears looking scared. When Knemon saw him he became very angry because a stranger had entered his field and grabbing a branch he run after him, shouting that he should have used a public road.

Hearing this Chaireas leaves, advising Sostratus to come back the next day, when the old man will hopefully be in a better mood. Sostratus stays there with his slave. Knemon appears, speaking to himself, and Pyrrhias runs away. The old man starts shouting at Chaireas, who also happens to be standing in his property. As an excuse he says that he has arranged to meet someone there. Knemon, still angry, returns to his house grumbling.

Myrrhine comes out of the house to bring water with the jug as Simike had accidentally thrown the bucket in the well. Sostratus fills up the jug, but as he is giving it to her they are seen by Gorgias' slave, her brother. The slave becomes suspicious and informs Gorgias, who as a result thinks that the young man is harassing his sister. As they talk, Sostratus passes by on his way to Knemon's house to talk to him. Gorgias accuses him of trying to seduce his sister. Sostratus informs him that he has fallen in love with her and he is going to ask from her father permission to marry her, even without any dowry, as he is rich. Gorgias is persuaded. He apologises to Sostratus and tells him that his old man has announced that he will only marry his daughter with someone like Knemon. He advises Sostratus to forget about Myrrhine, but Sostratus asks for his help. Gorgias proposes that they go to his field together as it is next to that of Knemon and Sostratus will be able to start a conversation with the old man. He must, however, be seen working in the field because if Knemon sees him idle and lazy, he will not like it. The young man accepts and they leave together.

Getas, a slave of Sostratus' father appears along with Sikon the cook, carrying food and items for a sacrifice to god Pan. Their lady saw a dream that Pan tied her son with ropes and forced him to work as a farmer in a field. She wanted to offer a sacrifice, so that the dream would not come true.

Knemon, watching the people arriving for the sacrifice, stays indoors complaining about the crowd. Sikon has forgotten the cauldron, necessary for the sacrifice. First Getas and then the cook ask Knemon to lend one to them. However, the old man scolds them and threatens to beat them.

Gorgias and Sostratus return, the latter utterly exhausted by the work. They had been waiting for Knemon in vain. Gorgias departs and Sostratus meets Getas. As soon as he hears of the sacrifice he goes to invite Gorgias and his slave to cajole them.

Knemon's old servant, Simike, comes out of their house. Knemon is running after her shouting that she stole his hoe. She tells him that she accidentally threw the bucket in the well and as she tried to retrieve it with the grub hoe she lost that too. The old man threatens to hang her and deciding to go to the well to retrieve his tools himself, he falls in.

Simike calls Gorgias for help and he in turn calls Sostratus. Gorgias immediately jumps into the well and Sostratus stands leaning over to pull the rope. He almost lost his grip three times, as he cannot take his eyes off the maiden who is weeping next to the well for her father.

Knemon finally emerges out of the well, having seen death before him. He now realises that Gorgias, whom he had always reprimanded, with great effort saved his life.. Deciding that he needs a helper, he calls him to stay with him and offers him half his property. He entrusts him with the duty to get Myrrhine married and announces that he gives to her the other half of his property as a dowry.

Gorgias immediately presents Sostratus as a suitor for Myrrhine. Knemon observes that he is tanned from the sun of that day which he spent working in the field for the first time in his life, and he concludes that he is a farmer. Nobody is eager to tell him the truth and he entrusts Gorgias with the technicalities of the marriage. Then Kallipides, Sostratus' father arrives in order to participate in the ritual of the family sacrifice.

Sostratus announces to his father that he is getting married and tries to persuade him to give his sister to Gorgias as a wife. Kallipides objects; it is too much for him to have both his son and his daughter married with poor people. However his son insists and he finally gives in. Gorgias, having heard everything, intervenes and refuses to marry a rich girl as he is poor. Kallipides, moved by the honesty of the young man, is now the one who insists in favour of this marriage. He offers a good dowry and at the same time refuses any dowry offer for his son.

They decide to organise a celebration for the night and that the double wedding should take place tomorrow. They

invite Knemon but as he refuses they send Getas to keep him
company. Getas, angry with Knemon for his attitude earlier
that day, calls the cook Sikon to exact their revenge. They
take him outside his house as he sleeps and start knocking
on the door in turns, shouting and asking from the owner to
borrow various things. The cook reprimands the old man; he
tells him that the other people do not need him, but instead
he is the one in need of others. A nice banquet is taking place,
with many dishes and beautiful maidens; he too should join
them in dancing. Getas and the cook threaten to drag him.
Finally Knemon half-heartedly accepts. They carry him on
their hands to the banquet, where they place a wreath on
his head.

THE FROGS
(ARISTOPHANES)

The beginning of this comedy takes place in front of the house of Hercules and continues in Hades. Dionysus, the god of wine, appears on the stage along with his slave Xanthias who is riding a donkey and carrying a bundle on his back. Dionysus is dressed in a ridiculous way: He is wearing an orange cloak and high-heeled shoes and over the cloak he has thrown a lion's skin very similar to that of Hercules. He is also holding a club similar to the Herculean one.

He knocks on the door. Hercules opens and seeing the way he is dressed bursts into laughter. Dionysus tells him that he wants to go to Hades, the World of the Dead, to bring Euripides back. He says he needs a great poet and none of them are alive anymore. He has dressed like this because he believes that he will receive assistance by those who helped Hercules, when he was on his way to Hades, which he had visited to bring back Cerberus – the monstrous three-headed dog who guarded the dead. The god asks Hercules to show him the best way to get there and Heracles answers that he must cross a bottomless lake in Charon's small boat (Charon was the ferryman of the dead). He would then reach a dirty and muddy place used for the immersion of the sinners, and finally he would reach a myrtle grove. From there the Initiates will lead him to the mansion of Pluto, the king of the dead.

A dead man passes by, on his own trip to Hades. Dionysus proposes to pay him to carry his bundle, but they cannot reach an agreement and the man leaves. Dionysus and Xanthias meet Charon; he agrees to carry the god across but refuses to accept a slave on his boat. The only option for Xanthias is to walk around the shores of the lake. Despite objections raised by Dionysus who claims he does not know how to row, Charon forces him to do so, telling him that the frogs will keep the beat.

As the boat moves, frog croaking can be heard but its beat is constantly changing, confusing Dionysus as he is trying to row. Dionysus shouts at them and finally the frogs fall silent. The god pays Charon with two ovoloi (the standard price of the ticket for this trip) and disembarks. They have arrived before Xanthias, so he waits for him. When his slave arrives they start walking together, and Xanthias scares the faint-hearted Dionysus with stories of imaginary monsters.

The whistling of flutes can be heard and the chorus, composed of the Initiates, approach talking and singing. When they meet the two travellers, they show Pluto's house to them. Dionysus knocks on the door. Aeacus, Pluto's porter, opens and asks who they are. Dionysus, dressed the way he is, replies that he is Hercules. Aeacus shouts at him and threatens him, reminding him that last time he descended to Hades he stole Cerberus. A fearful Dionysus asks Xanthias to swap clothes with him so that Xanthias can present himself as Hercules to the next person they meet. However, a servant-girl of Persephone appears and invites Xanthias to a rich supper with young girls dancing, thinking he is Hercules. Dionysus is not pleased and orders Xanthias to give him back the lion's skin and orders him to swap roles once again. Xanthias obeys.

But a new twist comes: two hostesses appear and upon seeing who they think is Hercules, threaten to bring charges against him because during his last trip he ate a lot of food but left without paying for it. Faced with this new situation the two visitors change clothing once again. Aeacus appears and calls his men to arrest who he thinks is Hercules. Xanthias defends himself and proposes to Aeacus, as the custom had it, to prove his innocence by interrogating his slave as harshly as possible. To avoid being tortured, Dionysus reveals the truth: That he is god Dionysus and Xanthias is his slave. Xanthias denies this and proposes to Aeacus to start torturing Dionysus, arguing that if he truly is a god and the son of Zeus, as he claims to be, he would not feel any pain. Dionysus proposes the opposite. Aeacus then starts beating both of them in turns. To convince him of their innocence, they try by any means to hide their pain. Aeacus gets confused and sends them to Pluto, for him and his wife Persephone to solve the puzzle and decide their fate accordingly.

A servant comes out of Pluto's house, together with Xanthias who is at last recognised to be a slave. A tumult is heard and the servant says that it is coming from an argument between Aeschylus and Euripides. While the throne of Tragedy in the underworld was being held by the former, when Euripides arrived he asked to take the throne by exhibiting his art. The spectators, being of disputable quality and morality, were delighted with the newcomer's ways and agreed to organise a contest which would decide the outcome regarding the throne. At the end of the contest, the servant says that they will "weigh" poetry on scales. Dionysus, being the most competent in such matters, has been appointed as the judge of the contest. The two slaves exit the stage.

The two contestants arrive and the contest begins. Euripides accuses Aeschylus of having started his plays with chorals, while his heroes were silent on stage for an unbearable amount of time; he also used incomprehensible words and phrases. He, on the contrary, used simpler words, he always began by having the hero narrate his genealogy and all his heroes had speaking roles, no matter how small. Aeschylus fights back, claiming that poetry should better people. He based his plays on heroic warriors, while Euripides' heroes were despicable. Euripides argues that what he wrote was factual, but Aeschylus insists that the poet must hide the evil, as by doing so he teaches the young.

Finally, Aeschylus asks for the scales to be used. In all three attempts his verses are proven to be heavier than those of Euripides. Dionysus hesitates to make a decision. Pluto reminds him of the reason of his visit to the Underworld; in addition to the decision about the throne, he is here to bring back on earth an important poet. Who will he choose? The god asks the poets their view on how Athens could be saved. Euripides proposes the change of the current leaders of the city in favour of others, who have been cast aside. Aeschylus proposes that the Athenians should forget about their fields and invade the enemy's land based on their navy, which should be financed from their riches, otherwise there is no point in having these.

Dionysus decides to take Aeschylus with him. Pluto organises a dinner in their honour and the play ends with the chorus bidding farewell to the travellers.

THE GIRL FROM SAMOS
(MENANDER)

Two houses, the house of Nikeratos and that of his friend Demeas, frame the stage. Out of the latter comes Moschion, the adopted son of the owner. He feels sorry he will upset his stepfather, who had always loved him. When Demeas and Nikeratos left for a long voyage in Pontos, Demeas' concubine, Chrysis of Samos, often kept company to the wife of Nikeratos. Moschion met and fell in love with Plagon, the daughter of Nikeratos, and they had a baby together. Moschion then promised to Plagon's mother he would marry her daughter as soon as the two fathers would return from their voyage. He took the baby in his house and, since the child of Chrysis who was pregnant at the time died, Chrysis nurses his child as if it were her own.

Now that both friends are back from their voyage, the son is ashamed and hesitant to tell his stepfather what has happened. Chrysis appears and Moschion tells her that it will probably be better if they present the baby as her own. She accepts, not fearing Demeas' wrath, as she is convinced that he loves her dearly. After this has been agreed Moschion goes in his room to rehearse what he will say to his stepfather.

Demeas and Nikeratos appear, talking about the things they saw in the faraway places they visited and of the advantages of Athens, but also about the wedding of their children which they decided on during their trip. Nikeratos leaves and Demeas learns about Chrysis' child. Moschion appears and his father tells him that following what he has just learned, he will expel Chrysis and her illegitimate child from his house. Moschion defends Chrysis by saying that she was probably raped and concludes that he must keep her because she evidently loves him. His father changes the subject and suggests to him that he should marry Plagon. Moschion accepts and declares his love for the girl. Demeas leaves at once and calls Nikeratos to come out of his house. Impulsively he tells him that he decided to set the wedding date for their children on that same day. Nikeratos finds that to be too soon and hesitates, but eventually accepts. Demeas immediately calls his slave Parmenon and orders him to start the preparations for the wedding.

In the next act, Demeas appears as if stricken by a thunderbolt. He overheard the old nurse of Moschion soothing the crying baby by saying that she had breastfed his father and ordering a young slave to wash the baby so that it will not be dirty on his father's wedding. Demeas had left quietly, but very suspicious. When he saw Parmenon he asked him if the baby was Moschion's child, adding that as a favour to him she is now nursing it. The slave, thinking that Demeas is aware of the truth, answers that what he says is true. A wrathful Demeas tries to beat Parmenon, who manages to run away. Left alone, the father tries to justify his son by putting all the blame on Chrysis, who must have seduced him. Always with the interests of his son in mind, he decides to expel Chrysis without revealing the true reason. He will just pretend that he got angry because of the baby. So he does, letting her have whatever she had earned during their relationship, together with female slaves; but he cannot resist telling her that she will now see how women of her kind live. He enters the house leaving Chrysis crying. When Nikeratos however learns his friend's behaviour, he feels compassion for her and takes her in his house until Demeas calms down.

In the next act, Nikeratos and Moschion approach Demeas in an attempt to make him change his mind. His son speaks first, asking him why he expelled Chrysis and trying to persuade him to keep her. Demeas tells him angrily Parmenon has revealed the truth to him and that he knows that he is the father of the baby; he tells him that this act is pure sacrilege and that he should not dare to even look at him in the eyes. Moschion, not understanding who he assumes to be the mother of the baby, tries to defend both himself but mainly Chrysis, for whom he insists that she bears no responsibility.

On hearing them, Nikeratos agrees with Demeas. He says that if he was unlucky that such shame fell on him, he would have disowned his son and sold Chrysis as a slave. He adds that he does not want to see him again. When Moschion and Demeas are left alone, the son realises his father's ignorance about the true mother and he clears up the situation.

Nikeratos returns disconcerted. He tells them that, upon entering his house, he saw his daughter breastfeeding the baby. Nikeratos' words are proof to Demeas that what Moschion has just revealed to him is the truth. Moschion, fearing the reaction of Nikeratos, goes inside. Demeas tries to calm his friend down, but in vain. Nikeratos enters his house and Demeas fears that in his wrath he may harm his grandchild. After a while Nikeratos comes out angry. Chrysis, he says, is holding the baby and is refusing to give it to him. When he enters again threatening to murder Chrysis, Demeas decides that the best thing to do is to reveal the full truth to him.

Chrysis runs out of the house chased, embracing the baby tightly and asking for help. Demeas intervenes and faces Nikeratos. By first asserting that his son has every intention to marry his daughter, he indirectly lets him understand who the true parents of the baby are. Finally, Nikeratos calms down and both fathers decide to prepare their houses for the wedding of their children. They go inside.

Moschion appears displeased by the accusations his father had unjustly expressed against him. He decides to shock him by faking his departure from home to fight as a mercenary. Parmenon appears, so Moschion sends him to bring him a cloak and a sword and expects to hear the entreaties of his stepfather when he hears about his supposed departure.

Parmenon returns, thinking that Moschion wants to leave, and tells him that inside the house his wedding is being prepared in a fast pace, something he appears not to be aware of. Despite Parmenon's warning, Moschion insists on having the cloak and sword brought to him, as he had ordered. Left alone, Moschion starts worrying lest his stepfather, in his anger, lets him leave.

Parmenon arrives bringing the cloak and the sword for Moschion. Demeas arrives too, having been notified by the slave. Demeas asks his son what is going on and, realising that Moschion was insulted, apologises to him. What was of most importance was that, when he learned that Moschion was the father of the baby, he concealed this fact so that their enemies would not rejoice. But if Moschion leaves for war, he would be acting as if there was something he was trying to avoid, so everything would be revealed and the family would be disgraced.

Nikeratos exits and, seeing Moschion ready for departure, he threatens him that he will not let him leave after having seduced his daughter. With the intervention of Demeas, so that Nikeratos will not be further angered, Moschion changes his mind. After that they all make their way to the wedding. With oaths, offerings, dances, wreaths and wishes for legitimate offspring, the wedding and the banquet take place and the comedy ends.

THE KNIGHTS
(ARISTOPHANES)

Two of elderly Demos' slaves[1], Nicias and Demosthenes[2], come out of his house. They speak of a new slave, Paphlagon, whose arrival in the house resulted in what was almost the daily beating of the remaining slaves. They wonder how they will get out of this situation. Demosthenes reports that Paphlagon flatters Demos and pretends he has done the work done by others. For example, a loaf of bread Demosthenes had prepared in Pylos was stolen by Paphlagon and served by him as his own. He also says that Paphlagon deceives his master with oracles.

---

1 Demos is the personification of the people (demos) of Athens. Demos in ancient greek means a. the common people, the sovereign people, the free citizens, b. municipal borough.

2 Nicias and Demosthenes were well-known Athenian generals. Paphlagon represents Cleon, a famous demagogue, former tanner and political enemy of Aristophanes, who is frequently ridiculed in his plays. Cleon had just gained enormous popular support after a military victory in Pylos; that victory was also the feat of Demosthenes, who had almost finished the military campaign before the arrival of Cleon.

Demosthenes suggests that Nicias should go and steal Paphlagon's oracles. Nicias agrees and comes back with an oracle about the succession of the city governors: the third governor is a tanner (Paphlagon) and he will be succeeded by a sausage seller. The two slaves think that, if they find a sausage seller, they will be saved. Indeed one appears, Agoracritus, advertising his goods. Demosthenes immediately announces to him that soon he will become the governor of Athens. Stunned, Agoracritus, insists that it must be a mistake, since he does not have either the appropriate education or ancestry. Demosthenes repeats that the qualifications he has are the ones needed for a politician. He promises him the support of one thousand horsemen or "knights" who comprise the chorus of the play and are against the tanner.

Paphlagon appears full of wrath, accusing them of conspiracy. Agoracritus gets scared and tries to run away, but Demosthenes holds him and calls the horsemen to assist them. The head of the chorus comes forward and starts blaming Paphlagon. Paphlagon in turn tries to flatter the horsemen, but their mind remains unchanged. Agoracritus then threatens Paphlagon with physical violence. He warns him that he will lodge a complaint against him on the grounds that he supplies the enemy's ships with food. The threats from one to the other continue. They both take pride on their indecency. The chorus head repeats that the sausage seller is indeed appropriate to take over Paphlagon's position, as he seems to share all the negative qualifications possessed by the city's politicians.

Paphlagon and Agoracritus try to persuade everybody for each one's superiority in dishonesty. In this competition, which also involves physical violence, Agoracritus is the winner. Paphlagon expresses his certainty that he is the victim of a conspiracy and runs to the people's Assembly in order to press charges against the conspirators. Agoracritus follows him in order to face him there too.

Agoracritus returns with the attitude of a winner. He says that Paphlagon went straight to the Assembly to denounce the horsemen as conspirators. When the Assembly was about to be persuaded, Agoracritus shouted as loudly as he could – that the sardines are now cheaper than they used to be. The members of the Assembly, whose first concern is their stomach, immediately started applauding him. Nobody was paying attention to what Paphlagon was saying after that moment. Agoracritus run in the market, bought leeks and coriander and offered a free salad with the sardines and ended up winning the Assembly's vote. Paphlagon joins him on the stage and they start accusing one another again. It is proposed that Demos should take the final decision. When he appears, they both start flattering him. Paphlagon asks for a gathering of the people in Pnyx, the hill upon which the Athenian Assembly held its meetings, so that Demos decides who is most loyal to him.

In that gathering Agoracritus accuses Paphlagon of rejecting all peace offerings, while Paphlagon replies that he does so because he wants Demos to be the ruler of all Greeks. Agoracritus counters that Paphlagon wants the war in order to be bribed by the allied cities. Demos falters. Agoracritus, wanting to cajole Demos, offers him a pair of shoes and a cloak as gifts. At once, Paphlagon offers his own leather jacket, which Demos does not accept. Paphlagon, however, refuses to give up; he asks Demos to listen to his oracles before taking the final decision. Agoracritus then announces that he too has some oracles to read. Each of the two opponents carries a package of oracles. Despite their attempts to attract Demos each to their side, they do not succeed, even after reading the obscure oracles. They are led to promises of wine and food offerings. They go to bring the offerings, leaving Demos alone with the chorus who criticise him for being prone to flattering. Demos reveals that he has become aware of the intentions of the two men and he is also pretending, taking advantage of the offerings that accompany their attempts. Finally, the contenders start giving him food. When the offerings are over, Agoracritus wins by proving he has offered to Demos all he had, while Paphlagon only offered him a small portion, keeping most of it for himself.

Agoracritus, as the winner, uses magic to revitalise Demos and bring back his old splendour of the Persian Wars period. Yet, he also reprimands him for being deceived by flatteries and choosing to spend his money on salaries for the Athenians instead of strengthening the navy. Demos acknowledges his mistake and feels bad. Agoracritus solaces him by reassuring him that the responsibility was not his; the impostors who influenced him are the ones to blame.

After that Demos, who has truly changed, reports various reparative measures he will implement in the future.

Agoracritus triumphantly presents a thirty-year peace treaty in the form of a beautiful maiden, who was being kept imprisoned by Paphlagon for a long time. It is decided that he must be punished for that, by doing the job of Agoracritus, which is selling sausages. Demos calls Agoracritus to the Prytaneion, while he orders that Paphlagon should wear the clothes of Agoracritus and should be placed at a point so that foreigners can see who was responsible for their torment.

THE WASPS
(ARISTOPHANES)

Two guards, Sosias and Xanthias, trying not to sleep, are talking in front of Philocleon's house, which is wrapped in a net. Bdelycleon, Philocleon's son is sleeping on the terrace. Xanthias informs us that their master Bdelycleon has ordered them to guard his father, so that he does not get out of the house The aged father suffers from a psychological disorder nobody has heard of: he has an obsession for trials. Up until now he has never missed a day in court in order to judge as part of the jury, and even before daybreak he is the first to run to secure a good seat.

His son has used various methods trying to heal him. First he discussed the issue with him, then he hid his coat so that he could not go out; he also put him in purgative baths, took him to the hospital, but to no avail. Then he decided that the only therapy would be to imprison him in their own house. For this not only he had to use two guards, but since his father is sly and always manages to escape, he had the whole house wrapped with the net.

Bdelycleon wakes up shouting that the slaves were not paying attention and his father got in the oven, trying to exit the house by passing through the chimney's pipe. His son heard a noise and asked who was inside. The answer from a voice inside the chimney was that it was the smoke. Bdelycleon closes the escape route. Philocleon, desperate, declares that if he does not convict at least one accused person, he will be disobeying an oracle by god Apollo, which will result in his death. In spite of the pleadings, Xanthias stops him and Philocleon threatens that he will tear the net with his teeth. Unfortunately, as Xanthias reminds him, he has no teeth.

Bdelycleon comes down from the terrace. Philocleon is hiding under his donkey in order to escape, but Bdelycleon grabs him and pushes him through the house's door, ordering Xanthias to pile up stones in front of it and lock it. After the guard has executed his orders, Bdelycleon goes in his room and Xanthias, tired, falls asleep.

The chorus of the comedy appears; it comprises of old men in the form of wasps. They are accompanied by children that hold lamps to light the way. The head of the chorus declares that their protector, Cleon, has sent them to judge Laches. He has told them to be in the court very early and be very angry with the accused. (Once more Aristophanes attacks Cleon, the powerful demagogue of ancient Athens. It is not by chance that the two main roles of the play are called Philo-Cleon and Bdely-Cleon, i.e. "Cleon-friendly" and "Cleon-detesting".)

Passing in front of Philocleon's house, the men of the chorus wonder what happened, as he did not come with them as he always did. Philocleon appears behind a small window. The chorus head exhorts him to come out quickly and Philocleon reveals that he has made a hole on the net by chewing slowly at it. Then the chorus head throws him a rope to grab and descend after he slips through the hole. Although Philocleon starts to descend slowly and silently, he is noticed by the guards and Xanthias hits him with branches to force him get back into his room.

Bdelycleon comes down from the terrace. The members of the chorus threaten him by showing their weapons, pointed as stings and ask to set Philocleon free. Bdelycleon does not yield to their demand; instead, he threatens the chorus with violence and the chorus men start to retreat. Eventually, father and son engage into a debate with the chorus members acting as arbitrators.

The father starts first, by stressing how significant is the power a position in the jury gives to an old man. Important people greet him respectfully by shaking his hand, while the accused beg him to set them free of charges and try to bribe him. When Bdelycleon asks him about the practical benefits, Philocleon says that the members of the jury enjoy the privilege not to render account to anyone; the bottom line is that they are the state themselves. But the most important argument in favour of this office is the salary of three *ovoloi* that they receive. The wasps of the chorus are delighted by his words.

Bdelycleon, estimating the public income at about 2,500 *talents* every year, says that public judges get in total 150 *talents* or less. The rest is going to the elected officials, who trap the poor people into voting for them. The three *ovoloi* given to the public judges have actually been earned by them when they were defending the state by fighting, either on a ship or in the infantry. However, in order to take them, they are ordered to go to the courts early, while the prosecutors, even if they come late, take six *ovoloi*. The chorus' convictions are shaken. Bdelycleon adds that the money should go to the veterans of war as a pension. He adds that he decided to close his father indoors, so that he will pass his time well, without being exploited. The chorus seem to be persuaded, Philocleon however has some objections. He capitulates, on the condition that he does not stop judging.

Bdelycleon proposes to establish a private court in the house, which will judge domestic matters. His father will not even lose his income, since he will be giving him the same salary. Philocleon accepts and the first trial is set. Accused is their dog Labes of Aexonia, because he snatched a piece of Sicilian cheese from the kitchen and ate it. Prosecutor is the other dog of the house, Cyon of the Cydathenea borough. (This satirises the fact that Cleon, a Cydathenea citizen, accused Laches from the Aexonia borough, the general of the Sicilian Expedition, of stealing public money during that expedition.) Two individuals come disguised as dogs. Cyon accuses Labes that he ate the piece of cheese alone and did not share it with him. He concludes his speech asking for the punishment of the accused, claiming "one bush cannot feed two thieves". Bdelycleon, acting as the defense, deceives his father making him throw his vote into the acquittal ballot box. When he realises that he acquitted the accused, Philocleon faints and when he comes round asks the gods for forgiveness, saying that this will be a burden on his soul. His son tries to relieve him from the guilt by promising to him a happy life, full of celebrations and feasts with much food.

Philocleon leaves the house followed by Bdelycleon and a slave. His son has dressed him in new clothes despite his objections, and has gives him lessons in good manners. He wants him to talk and behave like the rich. After the lesson, father and son walk away to attend a symposium. They take Xanthias with them, while the chorus stay on the stage and recite a choral.

Xanthias returns complaining for the beating he has received. He describes how Philocleon messed things up. He offended the guests with abusive teasing and now he is coming back from the dinner, drunk and beating whomever he meets. Philocleon appears singing, having a flute-playing girl with him and followed by some strangers. He threatens the strangers, while they, being his former fellow-diners, threaten in turn that they will lodge a complaint against him. Undaunted Philocleon replies that anything they say regarding trials is obsolete. He says that what is important in his life is now the flute-player and he turns to her while stroking her. The strangers finally go away, making threatening gestures. Philocleon is left alone with the young flute-player.

He addresses her with words of love. Soon, however, Bdelycleon approaches them running. Before he comes close, his father tells the girl to take his torch and stay motionless, pretending she is a statue. Bdelycleon reprimands his father for his erotic games, which are not appropriate for his age, and pointing to the girl accuses him of stealing her from the symposium. Philocleon denies this accusation, arguing that what his son is showing to him is a statue. Of course his son is not persuaded and pushes the girl into the house.

Several people arrive complaining and the old man mocks them. Bdelycleon, fearing that every minute that his father is left out of the house will result in another complaint against him, carries him inside.

Xanthias is seen coming out of the house; he says that the old man caused them new troubles. He drank again and was dancing all night long without a break. After a while Philocleon appears, still dancing a crazy dance. He boasts that he is the best dancer and, turning to the audience, invites whoever thinks is a good dancer to compete with him. Three dancers come out of the audience and the comedy ends with Philocleon and the dancers exiting, dancing.

THESMOPHORIAZUSAE
(ARISTOPHANES)

In front of tragic poet Agathon's house, Euripides is talking to his relative Mnesilochus. Euripides reveals that in the festival of Thesmophoria –an exclusively female Athenian festival in honour of Demeter and Persephone– women are going to decide how to exterminate him because his writings are usually against them. He has thought to ask Agathon to appear in the festival and speak in his favour.

Agathon comes out on an ekkyklema (a theatre machine) with effeminate appearance and attitude. As he explains, the manners of a poet should fit the style of his writing, and as he writes about women his mannerisms should be similar. Euripides asks him to appear during the Thesmophoria dressed as a woman in order to defend him. Agathon refuses and suggests to Euripides to go there himself. Hearing this, Mnesilochus volunteers to go and Euripides accepts. He disguises Mnesilochus using Agathon's clothes and shaves him. Mnesilochus asks Euripides to promise that, in the event of something going wrong, he will find a way to save him. Euripides takes an oath and they depart.

In the festival of Thesmophoria women are gathered,

forming the chorus of the comedy. Mnesilochus is present. First a woman asks for a supplication to the gods. After the supplications of the chorus, she names a series of cases that are worthy of curse. The case of Euripides and his writings against women is listed amongst them. The other participants agree; the middle day of Thesmophoria is set as decision day on the kind of suitable punishment for Euripides who is found guilty by the women's unanimous opinion.

A woman mentions the evil Euripides has brought to them. He pulls them in the mud with his accusations. He writes that they drink, that they are unfaithful to their husbands and gives a detailed account of their deeds. As a result their husbands are now suspicious and search for indications they would have never thought of otherwise. They have put locks to the storehouses and dogs to the women's quarters to guard them from their lovers. Euripides is responsible for all this and they must find a way to annihilate him, probably with poison. The women of the chorus agree.

A second woman speaks. She says that she makes wreaths to sell to people who sacrifice to the gods. But since Euripides proclaimed in his tragedies that there are no gods, the sacrifices have almost completely stopped and her sales are half of what they used to be. She too proposes to punish him heavily.

The turn of Mnesilochus comes. He agrees with the previous speakers, adding however some extenuating circumstances. There had been several times when Euripides did not reveal indecencies. "She" makes reference to "her" personal experiences: being married for three days, she left her bed and went to meet a former lover. She adds that the poet has also not mentioned the many cases of adultery between them and their slaves. They are dishonest and they tell lies; is Euripides the one to blame? They deserve what they get.

The chorus gets suspicious. What is the agenda of the last speaker? They should punish her for what she said. Mnesilochus resists and speaks about freedom of speech. His words irritate the women and one of them physically attacks him. They stop when someone comes running; it is Cleisthenes, an effeminate Athenian, dressed as a woman. He informs them that he heard in the marketplace that Euripides has sent a relative of his in disguise to hear what was said and to learn of their decision. The women decide to search among them; Mnesilochus cannot answer their questions. They decide to take off his clothes in order to look at his genitals, and the fraud is revealed. Cleisthenes runs to the Prytaneion to inform the officials of the sacrilege. Mnesilochus grabs a baby from the hands of the first woman and, holding it at knife-point, threatens to kill the child. The chorus starts wailing and threaten to burn him alive. Mnesilochus unfolds the baby's swaddles only to discover that there is no baby, just a skin bag containing wine. He slices the bag with the knife and the wine starts flowing. The "mother" pretends to weep for her child; he gives her a cup of "blood" but finally pours it on the ground.

The play continues by showing the various attempts of

Mnesilochus to escape, all inspired by Euripidean tragedies. Mnesilochus, in an attempt to inform Euripides to come and save him, takes votive tablets (as in the tragedy *Palamedes*, only there the hero was in the sea and he had used oars), carves letters to Euripides on them and throws them around him. After that, he sits next to the altar to wait for his saviour.

In the meantime, the chorus praise women highly, comparing their abilities with those of men. They say that women are always accused even for minor things, while men get away with very serious crimes – even stealing public money.

As Euripides does not appear, Mnesilochus decides to try the tragedy *Helen* in order to confuse the women: He pretends to be Helen of Troy on the banks of Nile, waiting for her husband Menelaus. Soon "Menelaus" comes, in the form of Euripides. "Helen" and "Menelaus" recognise each other and she asks her husband to take her away from this city, where the king wants to marry her against her will, as she is faithful to Menelaus. However the women are not deceived and they do not let Mnesilochus leave. At that moment, a magistrate comes with a Scythian archer as his guard and Euripides runs away.

The magistrate orders the Scythian to tie the impostor to a phalanx and the women begin the holy ceremony of the Thesmophoria. Mnesilochus moans from the pain, begging the guard to loosen the rope a bit; instead he fastens him more tightly and leaves to bring a mattress to rest on.

Euripides returns disguised as Perseus, so Mnesilochus plays the role of Andromeda, the maiden liberated by Perseus when she was tied to a rock. Euripides alternates between the roles of Echo and Perseus. He tries to influence the archer to set his relative free but is unsuccessful and leaves; he returns after a while undisguised, together with a flute-player and a female dancer. He proposes peace to the women. He will never again speak or write a bitter word against them if they liberate the detained. If they refuse, though, he threatens that he will reveal many of their secrets to their husbands as soon as they return from the war. The women agree; only the Scythian remains to be persuaded.

Then Euripides gets dressed as an old woman, approaches the guard and tells the dancer to take off her blouse; in order to untie her sandals he sits her on the Scythian. The archer gets enthusiastic, but Euripides asks her to leave. The Scythian begs for just a kiss and the poet asks for money. The guard gives him his quiver with the arrows inside as a pledge and leaves with the girl for the kiss. Euripides then takes the opportunity to set Mnesilochus free. When the archer returns he searches for the prisoner and his arrows but in vain. The head of the chorus sends him at the opposite direction and the comedy ends.

WEALTH
(ARISTOPHANES)

Chremylus appears on the stage along with his slave
Carion who is complaining that from the moment his
master left the Delphi Oracle, they have been pointlessly
following an old blind man dressed in rags. Chremylus finally
answers the slave's persistent questions. He tells him that in
the oracle he asked Phoebus (the god Apollo) whether it
would be better for his son to become unjust and dishonest,
as nowadays those who have these characteristics live a
better life. The god told him to follow the first person he
would meet after he had left the premises of the Oracle and
to take him in his house. Both master and slave have been
asking the blind man who he is, but he refuses to tell them.
Finally, when they threaten to kill him, he reveals that he
is Wealth, an announcement they have difficulty to believe.
He explains that Zeus has blinded him out of jealousy for
humans, so that he cannot see who is just and honest and go
with them.

Chremylus tells him that he is honest and asks him to
come to his house, promising him that he will restore his
vision. Wealth refuses to be healed because he is afraid of

Zeus, the leader of the gods, but Chremylus persuades him by telling him that the reason Zeus is worshipped is because people ask from him to make them rich. If Wealth does not give Zeus the means to do that, Zeus will lose all his power. Wealth hesitantly accepts and Chremylus sends Carion to the peasants who form the comedy's chorus to ask them for help; if they succeed, they too will become rich.

After a while, Carion returns followed by the peasants who promise Chremylus all the help he needs when they learn about the Wealth. Back in Athens, Blepsidemus, a friend of Chremylus who learned that his friend suddenly became rich, appears on stage. Hearing the obscure explanations of Chremylus, he suspects him of foul play. Chremylus informs him that he has Wealth in his house, but that he is blind. It is necessary to heal him and he has decided to bring him to the temple of Asclepius.

As they prepare to leave, a repulsive woman arrives. She is Penia, the personification of poverty. A debate starts amongst them; Chremylus argues that if Wealth could see again, not only will the honest people become rich, but also the dishonest ones will become honest in order to become rich. Penia responds that if everybody gets rich, all arts and professional knowledge will be lost, since nobody will want to work anymore. Eventually, as nobody will want to work for another person, everyone will be forced to satisfy their own needs by doing all the jobs, even the most difficult ones. Chremylus objects by saying that the life of the poor is not desirable for the poor themselves. Penia responds that one must not confuse poverty with beggary; the beggar lacks everything, while the poor man works and acquires what he does not have. This way he also exercises his body, contrary to those who have wealth and are struck by illness caused by their inactivity. She adds that poor people are accompanied by modesty; but when these same people become rich, they lose all modesty and become unjust.

Neither of the men change their mind; they drive away the goddess of poverty, take Wealth and leave. Later on, Carion appears and announces to the chorus that Wealth's vision has been fully restored. Asclepius healed him, confirming how great a doctor he is. The chorus is delighted with the news they hear.

The wife of Chremylus comes out of the house and Carion explains to her everything that has happened. They first bathed Wealth and made sacrifices, laid him down upon the altar and went to sleep. But Carion was sleepless from his craving to eat the gruel an old woman had brought with her; so he witnessed Asclepius with his two daughters healing Wealth using two large snakes which looked to Carion to be licking the blind man's eyes.

Wealth is on his way home, but he is delayed by the people he meets on the way. The honest people, poor up to that day, greet him joyfully, while the rich ones whose properties had been amassed with fraud are now full of sorrow. Chremylus is annoyed by all his so-called "friends", who are now greeting him cordially because they have been told about Wealth. He enters his house with Wealth, while Carion comes out, expressing to the audience his satisfaction that the house is now full of goods. The cheap kitchenware was replaced by copper pieces and the fish plates were now silver.

A man appears followed by a boy; he is holding an old cloak and a pair of worn shoes. He says that once he was very rich and was helping those in need, but when he lost his fortune, those he had helped did not even want to speak to him. But now that he has become rich again being one of the honest men, he has come here to honour Wealth by offering him his old clothes.

Next, an informer comes in, complaining that he has lost everything, while his job is to support the law and protect the state interests in legal cases. His words cannot persuade of his good intentions, so Carion punishes him by taking his cloak and shoes, and giving him the old clothes of the honest rich person to wear. The informer leaves threatening that Wealth will have to face the consequences of subverting democracy with his acts.

Chremylus comes out of the house as an old woman dressed in gaudy colours arrives. She complains of being miserable. Up until now her relationship with a much younger man was fine; he was visiting her frequently and was doing everything she asked for in order to please her; she was offering him gifts, while he was even jealous of her. But from the moment Wealth's vision was restored, his attitude has changed and her former companion pays no attention to her any more. While Chremylus and the old woman are talking, the young man arrives. He says he has brought a wreath to offer to Wealth. Upon meeting his old lover, he insults her. Chremylus reprimands him, but also jeers at the old woman by calling her a "girl".

They all enter the house, leaving only the chorus on stage. The god Hermes arrives; he says that Zeus is very angry, because since Wealth was healed, all sacrifices have stopped. Carion objects; the reason for this is that Zeus was governing them in a very bad way. Meanwhile Hermes has smelled roasted meat and asks for some. As Hermes is interested only in his personal well-being, he decides not to return to the other gods and asks if the people will let him stay with them. Carion refuses, but Hermes insists: he will do any job they want in order to stay there. Carion finally accepts his offer and sends him to wash intestines so he can prove that he knows how to work. They enter the house together.

Finally, a priest of Zeus' arrives hungry, since no one makes sacrifices anymore, as everyone is rich and they do not need to ask the gods for any material goods. He asks permission to stay with them, as Hermes has done before him. Chremylus allows him to stay, revealing to him the most amazing news one could ever wish to hear: even Zeus himself has come to his house. He adds that now they will perform a ceremony to settle Wealth in his old position, at the back side of the temple of Athena, where the public money was being kept. They all leave for the ceremony. They are also followed by the old woman, who is happy as Chremylus has made a promise to her that the young man will visit her in the evening.

www.ingramcontent.com/pod-product-compliance
Lightning Source LLC
Chambersburg PA
CBHW030923090426
42737CB00007B/294